# UNEXPLAINED
# MYSTERIES OF THE
# ANCIENT WORLD

# UNEXPLAINED MYSTERIES OF THE ANCIENT WORLD

## EXTRAORDINARY ENIGMAS FROM HISTORY

**WILLIAM POTTER**

This edition published in 2025 by Arcturus Publishing Limited
26/27 Bickels Yard, 151–153 Bermondsey Street,
London SE1 3HA

AD011626UK

Printed in the UK

# CONTENTS

## CHAPTER 4: LOST IN TIME

## CHAPTER 5: RITUAL TRACES

# INTRODUCTION

Everyone loves a good mystery, whether it's a riddle, a code, a lost treasure or an unsolved murder – and the more ancient it is, the more enigmatic and enthralling it can be. Within this book, we investigate some of the most famous and unusual mysteries from history, including several that have captivated readers and audiences for thousands of years. Some even predate written historical records. For those, all we have are stones, carvings and inscriptions to ponder. In some cases there is text that has never been deciphered, or else there is little, but just enough, to draw us in.

Some of the mysteries recounted here are based on legends: shady, half-remembered tales that fascinate down the centuries, not only because of their historical and emotional resonance but because they are often based on some element of fact. Who is to say that there was not a real Queen of Sheba, a court of King Arthur, or a tribe of fierce Amazons joining wars against the Greeks? Even without archaeological evidence, so much has been written of these characters that there must have been an original inspiration, a memory, a song, or an oral tradition from which they sprang. In this book, we'll examine the first mentions of these subjects and weigh up their accuracy. We will look at how the myths developed and how they were understood through different ages, and consider the proofs and hypotheses offered over time.

These mysteries have lasted for millennia. Could Plato have imagined that the story he shared of Atlantis – ancient to him, having supposedly occurred 9,300 years before his own lifetime –

would be revisited in new tales thousands of years later? Would he have been gratified, or maybe incredulous, that scholars would be arguing over its veracity and location in the 21st century? Similarly, the mysterious writer and artist who created the perplexing Voynich Manuscript might have been entertained by the number of cryptologists who have laboured over its coded text for decades, trying to find patterns or clues that might help them understand its message – if, indeed, it even has one. Some of these mysteries may be deliberate hoaxes but they retain their fascination nonetheless. One can only admire the skill of their creators in producing a manuscript or relic so convincing that it has split opinion for centuries.

Several mysteries involve disappearances. What happened to the Neanderthals: were they killed or outcompeted by *Homo sapiens*? The wife of Tutankhamun was seemingly erased from the records on tomb and temple walls – was this disappearance actually an essential clue in his story? And, later in Egyptian history, another enduring conundrum is what happened to the body of Cleopatra. Was it a political decision to conceal her tomb or are we just looking for it in the wrong place? Was an entire legion of the mighty Roman Empire's soldiers wiped out in Scotland or the forests of Germany? The minimal archaeological or written evidence available for such long-distant events has generated no shortage of theories, including those involving conspiracies, to consider.

As for murders, there are several ancient cold cases worth re-examining. Tutankhamun, the subject of the 20th century's greatest archaeological find and perhaps one of history's best-known mysteries, was discovered with wounds on his skull, chest and leg. Were these the result of damage during mummification, or removal from his tomb, or are they evidence of foul play? Was Ötzi, a 5,000-year-old figure defrosted in the Alps, another murder victim? Modern forensics, CAT scans and DNA tests can unlock the secrets of these ancient corpses and even tell us what a victim's last meal was, and where it came from. But can they solve a crime several millennia old?

While some of the following mysteries do seem to have been solved, or at the very least new discoveries and advances in humankind's knowledge have seen off some of the more far-fetched contentions, many others remain a challenge. This is part of their allure, something that invites historians, archaeologists and armchair detectives to return to them again and again. Maybe there's something that others have missed or something far too outlandish to be taken seriously.

Or, maybe, the truth is that we don't want an answer. These mysteries of the ancient world are so absorbing that a definitive solution would spoil a game that has been played for thousands of years, and probably turn out to be somewhat mundane. There is an Atlantis in our imagination: could one discovered on the seabed match the image we already have of an ancient yet spectacularly advanced civilization? Would Stonehenge lose its magic if it turned out to be a collection of simple gravestones? Will pilgrims turn away from the Shroud of Turin or the chapel of the Ark of the Covenant because they are told that their relics are fabricated? The truth is, probably not. Everyone loves the enjoyable frustration that comes from a mystery that could have a dark human emotion, a fiendishly clever motivation, or maybe even a supernatural force behind it. Long may they intrigue.

# CHAPTER 1
# LOST CIVILIZATIONS

Legends tell us of many ancient cultures that have been buried or erased by conflict or cataclysm: of sunken Atlantis and Mu, of Minoan mazes and the wealthy African kingdoms of Sheba and Great Zimbabwe. But how many of these stories are myths and how much is based on real events and once-vital communities? Scouring the written record and archaeological traces provides surprising evidence that many of these fabled realms may actually deserve a place on the map of history.

Mystifying ruins and effigies bear witness to abandoned lands in the Indus Valley (in modern-day Pakistan and northern India) and Easter Island in the south-eastern Pacific Ocean. Who established these settlements and what caused their decline and eventual abandonment? The accounts that do exist reveal often-tragic stories of environmental degradation, climate change, abduction and disease, which may have been responsible for the mass migrations or disappearances of communities. In this way, the chronicles of the past provide sobering lessons for the future.

# DID ATLANTIS EXIST?

Said to be an island continent inhabited by a powerful civilization that was destroyed and submerged in antiquity as punishment for its hubris, Atlantis has inspired literature, films, and both serious investigation and far-fetched theories. Was it no more than a fictional example created to serve a philosophical discourse, or was there actually an ancient island nation named Atlantis, or a similar state, that inspired the enduring legend?

The first mention of Atlantis dates to between 359 and 347 BCE, when it was recorded in the works of the philosopher Plato. Plato was an ancient Greek born around 428 BCE, who founded a philosophical school in Athens and developed his ideas through reasoned argument. His dialogues, *Timaeus* and *Critias*, describe debates between Plato's teacher, Socrates, and his students. One debate centres around how a perfect society might behave while at war with other, flawed states. The politician Critias takes up the baton and recounts a story he describes as 'strange, though certainly true' of how Athens came into conflict with an advanced and expansionist city 9,300 years earlier. Through this dialogue, Plato sought to compare an ideal state – namely, early Athens – with its antithesis, a predatory civilization Critias called Atlantis.

The legend of Atlantis had already undergone a convoluted journey that risked variation and misinterpretation, even before Critias shared it with Socrates. According to the dialogues, Critias claimed to have heard the tale of Atlantis from his 90-year-old grandfather (also named Critias) who heard it from his father

Dropides after it was shared by Solon, an Athenian Greek legislator (and distant relative of Plato). Solon, in turn, received it from priests during a visit to Sais in Egypt, between 590 and 580BCE. The Egyptian priests scoffed at the Athenian's limited knowledge of his own nation's deep history. They told him of a time many thousands of years before, when Athens was led by a warrior class. This ancient Athenian society came into conflict with Atlantis, 'a mighty host, which, starting from a distant point in the Atlantic Ocean, was insolently advancing to attack the whole of Europe, and Asia to boot'.

Atlantis was described as a vast island continent positioned west of the Pillars of Heracles (Hercules), two rocky promontories that today connect the Atlantic Ocean and Mediterranean Sea at the Strait of Gibraltar. Larger than Libya and Asia Minor combined, Atlantis was supposed to have been founded by Poseidon, the Greek god of the sea and earthquakes, for his human lover Cleito. Cleito bore Poseidon ten sons. One of these was Atlas, who became the most powerful of the island's kings. For a time Atlas, his brothers and their descendants ruled Atlantis in a virtuous manner. However, as their divine blood thinned out these rulers became corrupt and arrogant.

## A WEALTHY AND SOPHISTICATED CIVILIZATION

The island of Atlantis was described in detail in Plato's dialogues. The north was mountainous, while the south featured a great plain over 550 km (340 miles) across. The island was rich with ores, fresh water and wildlife, including elephants. At its heart was the palace and city of Atlas. This featured a silver-and-gold temple dedicated to Poseidon, which was three times the size of the Athenian Parthenon. Within the temple was a statue of the sea god as tall as the Statue of Liberty and its pedestal.

The city of Atlas was surrounded by circles of land divided by three moats. These rings of earth were fortified by walls plated with bronze, tin and orichalcum, a valuable golden-yellow metal. Bridges crossed the moats and led northward, while tunnels and canals allowed ships to sail directly to the city's heart.

From here, the navies of Atlantis ventured into the Mediterranean and claimed Libya. They went on to establish an empire that incorporated parts of Egypt and Etruscan Italy, enslaving the defeated populations. According to the Egyptians, via Critias, the Atlanteans' expansion was eventually pushed back by a rebellion led by Athenians, before 'there occurred violent earthquakes and floods; and in a single day and night of misfortune all your warlike men in a body sank into the earth, and the island of Atlantis in like manner disappeared in the depths of the sea'. Atlantis, its people and armies, and the Athenian forces, were all wiped out. This cataclysm was said to be a punishment inflicted by the gods on Atlantis for its unforgivable hubris. According to Critias, the evidence of the island's subsidence was an impassable shoal of mud in the Atlantic Ocean.

If, as the Egyptians recounted, this disaster occurred 9,300 years before Plato, it would place Atlantis at least 6,000 years before pharaonic Egypt. This was a time when hunter-gatherers were beginning to cultivate wild cereals in the Levant, the last great Ice Age was ending, and mammoths still roamed Siberia. This version of Atlantis would have been far in advance of any established culture.

The account of Atlantis was considered improbable even in Plato's lifetime. His ex-pupil, the philosopher Aristotle, is said to have dismissed it as a fiction that was invented solely to make a point about governance. This is how it was understood for centuries, with very few writers repeating Critias's assertion that the fate of Atlantis was 'certainly true'. There are no existing mentions of an island called Atlantis west of Europe in the classical period, except in reference to Plato's discourse.

## EUROPEAN EXPLORATION REIGNITES INTEREST

All of Plato's Greek texts, except *Timaeus*, were lost to western Europeans until Latin translations were made in the 15th century. While European scholars were once again reading about Atlantis, the maps used by Christopher Columbus on his voyages to the New World showed no indication of an impassable Atlantean mud bank as described by Critias. Whether or not Columbus knew of

An artist's conception of Atlantis based on Plato's description.

Plato's works, the explorer had no expectation of finding Atlantis (although he was inspired by the imaginative 13th-century travel diaries of Marco Polo). The discovery of a new continent at the end of the 15th century, however, would inspire many to make a direct connection with Plato's concept.

Francisco López de Gómara, a priest and historian who wrote a sanitized account of the Spanish conquest of the New World, was one of the first to join the dots. In the 1550s he suggested that the Americas were Atlantis and that its indigenous peoples were descendants of Atlantean survivors. The discovery of monumental cities, pyramids, complex agricultural methods and astronomical records in Aztec and Mayan culture astonished European conquerors. They sought to take credit away from these ancient indigenous civilizations by claiming they had Caucasian influences. These ideas smacked of racial superiority.

The tale of Atlantis influenced several fictional and academic works in the following centuries, including Sir Thomas More's satire *Utopia* (1516), which positioned his ideal island in the New World. The English polymath Francis Bacon began work on *New Atlantis* around 1626. His unfinished novel, published posthumously, imagined the island of Bensalem off the coast of Peru. This island of scholars focused on scientific enquiry and bears comparison with London's 17th-century Royal Society. In 1679, Olaus Rudbeck, a professor of medicine at Uppsala University in Sweden, published a much-derided four-volume treatise, *Atland eller Manheim* (*Atlantica*). His work traced the origin of words and concluded that Sweden was the original location of Atlantis and, indeed, the cradle of civilization. Apart from these notable exceptions, Atlantis remained a minority interest for centuries. That was all to change at the end of the 19th century.

## ATLANTIS AS THE SOURCE OF MAJOR CULTURES

The idea that Mesoamerican cultures were inspired by Atlantis was revisited in the mid-1800s by the French writer Charles-Étienne Brasseur de Bourbourg, the American archaeologist Edward Herbert Thompson and the British-American antiquarian Augustus Le Plongeon. Their theories were absorbed into the beliefs known as 'Mayanism', which propose ancient contact between the Maya and Atlanteans and, as espoused in later theories, also with extraterrestrial visitors.

The writings of Brasseur de Bourbourg and Le Plongeon motivated a progressive American congressman named Ignatius Donnelly to publish his own thesis. An amateur historian of Irish stock, Donnelly had unsuccessfully attempted to help set up a utopian community in Minnesota. He shared the presumption that the pre-Columbian cultures of South America must have inherited many of their ideas from abroad, and published his evidence in *Atlantis: The Antediluvian World* in 1882.

Donnelly's proof for what he called 'diffusionism', or the tracing of noteworthy cultures back to a single source, was flimsy. For example, there was little similarity between artistic and architectural styles found on either side of the Atlantic that might suggest communication thousands of years ago. Where Plato had imagined Atlantis as a mercenary state – the anthesis of an ideal Athens – Donnelly saw it as a benign culture, spreading its advanced wisdom worldwide. Indeed, he went further, claiming Atlantis was the birthplace of civilization, that the Greek, Hindu and Scandinavian gods were Atlantean royalty, and that the deluge that destroyed Atlantis was the origin of all ancient flood myths. Donnelly's ideas inspired later 'pseudoarchaeological' works, which imagined surviving Atlanteans guiding cultures around the world, sharing their knowledge of agriculture, architecture and astronomy.

Among Donnelly's supporters was Helena Petrovna Blavatsky, a Russian-American mystic known as Madame Blavatsky. She claimed, without proof, that her 1888 work *The Secret Doctrine* was based on Atlantean texts transmitted to her during trances. The American clairvoyant Edgar Cayce, who forged a career as 'The Sleeping Prophet' by providing thousands of psychic readings, also believed in the existence of Atlantis. He claimed that the island had been powered through crystals and had developed a death ray. His prediction that Atlantis would be discovered in 1969 was just one of many outlandish notions presented without evidence.

These 'new-age' ideas of Atlantis were generally harmless. However, the contention that Atlanteans were a superior race that seeded future cultures would become popular with leading members of the German Nazi Party, who propagated their own theory of an Aryan master-race.

## SEARCHING FOR THE 'LOST' ISLAND

As theories about the importance and influence of Atlantis spread and evolved, the search for the location of the physical island continued. The possibility of a lost land bridge between Europe and America has been raised for centuries to explain similarities in animal and plant life on both sides of the Atlantic. This idea was supplanted in the mid-20th century, when the German meteorologist Alfred Wegener shared his theory of continental drift. This revealed how the continents had moved apart over millions of years, thanks to what we now know as plate tectonics. The jigsaw pieces of the continents could be slotted neatly into place and there was no need – or space – for a lost Atlantis to fill a gap.

In his book *The Secret of Atlantis* (1954), the German engineer Otto Muck provided compelling evidence that Atlantis once stood along the Mid-Atlantic Ridge, and was destroyed by an asteroid collision at 8 pm on 5 June, 8498BCE, leaving behind only the Azores islands (a Portuguese archipelago in the North Atlantic Ocean). He interpreted a row of undersea volcanoes as evidence of a sunken continent, which were later revealed to be the result of more recent faults in Earth's crust dividing the continental plates.

If there was no evidence in the Atlantic Ocean, perhaps Plato had provided the wrong co-ordinates. While the Pillars of Heracles are today understood to be the rocks that flank the Strait of Gibraltar, in Plato's time they may have marked a boundary within the Mediterranean, such as the Strait of Messina between Sicily and mainland Italy. Equally, Plato's Atlantic was not necessarily the ocean that bears the name today.

Many attempts were made to locate Atlantis, some naming sites far from the Strait of Gibraltar. Contenders have included Antarctica, Bolivia, Doggerland in the North Sea, South Africa, Türkiye, Germany, Malta and the Caribbean.

The volcanic island of Thera in the southern Aegean Sea was a major contender. Known today as the Greek holiday hotspot of Santorini, in 1450BCE Thera was a large island conveniently positioned between Cyprus and Crete, and a centre for trading and processing copper. At some point in time between 1620 and 1530BCE there was a major volcanic eruption (estimated to be at least four times as violent as the eruption of Krakatoa in Indonesia in 1883), which caused earthquakes and tsunamis. The major settlement at

Akrotini was buried under ash and the volcano collapsed, leaving a mostly submerged caldera (large crater) in the western part of today's Santorini, and a handful of other small islands.

Crete, 120 km (75 miles) south of Thera, has also been posited as a potential Atlantis. Like Thera, it had a thriving and advanced culture before the same volcanic disaster also brought it to ruin. Archaeologists have uncovered impressive palaces, highly sophisticated ceramics and frescoes which could match descriptions of a sophisticated culture presented by Plato. Associated with the story of King Minos, this civilization is now labelled as Minoan (page 45) and evidence of its reach has been uncovered as far away as Sicily. Nothing was known about the Minoan civilization during Plato's time, although it is possible that knowledge of the catastrophic volcano reached the philosopher and inspired his tale.

As for Plato's 9,300-year timescale, there are several examples of Plato being unreliable with figures. The suggestion that Stone-Age Athens had anything like the weaponry and military might needed to match Atlantis as described is not supported by any archaeological evidence. It has been suggested that the thousands of years that Solon quoted are a result of his misreading of Egyptian hieroglyphs, and that the number 9,300 actually refers to seasons or months. One revised date for an Atlantean–Athenian war is around 1200BCE, placing it within 50 years of the Trojan War (the conflict between early Greeks and Troy, or modern-day Anatolia, Türkiye). Similarly, the scale of Atlantis and its million-strong army is also likely to be an exaggeration. If Atlantis existed, it was more likely an island rather than a continent and rather than one nation, Atlantis was more probably a coalition of states in the central Mediterranean.

While the idea of such an advanced society and the disappearance of a vast area of land seems fanciful (at least prior to Krakatoa), the story of Atlantis may have been inspired by verified cataclysms centuries before Plato's birth. Plato almost certainly experienced or knew of such events in his lifetime. One such was the destruction of the Greek polis Helike due to earthquake and soil liquefaction in 373 BCE, when Plato would have been around 53 years old. This city-state also had a temple dedicated to its patron, Poseidon, matching Plato's Atlantis. Centuries later, Greek and Roman travellers would report seeing submerged ruins and a statue of Poseidon. The ruins of Helike, lost for more than a millennium, were rediscovered by archaeologists in 2001, in an ancient lagoon near the village of Rizomylos.

It is tempting to magnify the reports of cataclysms around the Mediterranean during Plato's lifetime and stories of half-forgotten pre-Hellenic powers – but transforming Thera, Crete or Helike into Atlantis is wishful thinking. They fail to match the age, location, scale or grandeur of Plato's lost continent. Considering the lack of independent reports, Plato's Atlantis, as described in his dialogues, seems entirely to be an invention of the philosopher. Plato used Atlantis to illustrate a scenario involving an 'ideal' state (Athens) and its nemesis (Atlantis). This conclusion is supported by the lack of convincing references to the island-continent, the absence of archaeological or geological evidence from oceanic mapping, and the impossibility of a missing continent fitting neatly into the jigsaw of continental plates.

All attempts to position Atlantis away from Plato's setting seem contrived. Yet, while a technologically advanced continent of empire-builders from the Atlantic Ocean may not have existed, events that inspired Plato to concoct his myth are worthy of investigation. Excavations of Helike, Santorini and Crete provide fascinating glimpses of cultures destroyed by 'acts of God'. And whether or not Atlantis existed, Plato's lesson that pride comes before a fall is no less potent without its fantastical illustration.

# WAS THERE A QUEEN OF SHEBA?

The Queen of Sheba has captured imaginations for centuries. Her brief encounter with King Solomon in the Bible has been fleshed out as a full-blown romance in poetry, literature and cinema. Claimed by both Arabian and African traditions, the queen has been portrayed as a femme fatale and revered as the matriarch of a major African dynasty. Her image is carved into stone reliefs and cast in bronze on the doors of some of Europe's major cathedrals, and is depicted on relics treasured by millions of Ethiopian pilgrims. How much of this biblical romance is history and, more importantly, was there a true Queen of Sheba?

According to the Old Testament's Book of Kings, the Queen of Sheba was one of many rulers of the ancient world who made the journey to Jerusalem in the 10th century BCE to pay their respects to King Solomon, the ruler of Israel who was renowned for his wisdom. This unnamed queen delivered great gifts, including 'camels that bore spices and very much gold, and precious stones'. She tasked the king with questions and riddles, which Solomon answered to her satisfaction, after which she returned home.

The queen's story is elaborated in the *Targum Sheni*, an Aramaic embellishment of the Hebrew Book of Esther, and repeated in the Qur'an. Here, Solomon – who can communicate with birds – was informed by a hoopoe of a kingdom named Sheba, led by a queen who worshipped the sun as a god. The bird was sent to Kitor in Sheba with a letter requesting the presence of the queen. She responded extravagantly, sending many ships bearing gifts and 6,000 youths of the same height, all born at the same hour, and dressed in purple. They heralded her arrival within three years.

When the Queen of Sheba finally arrived at Solomon's palace in Jerusalem, she entered a hall with a glass floor that she mistook for water. The queen lifted the hem of her skirt to avoid getting it wet, revealing hairy legs. This chapter was expanded in an Arabic version, which had one of the queen's legs exposed as that of a goat, being hairy and cloven. Suspecting the queen's imperfection, Solomon had arranged the reflective floor to confirm it. He also concealed a piece of wood from the sacred Temple of Jerusalem for the queen to step across. When the queen did so, her disfigured leg was magically repaired.

According to Josephus, the 1st-century BCE Roman-Jewish historian, the Queen of Sheba was queen of both Egypt and Ethiopia. She delivered the first specimens of a medicinal balsam that grew in Jerusalem in the historian's lifetime.

## THE AFRICAN TRADITION: MAKEDA

The most detailed and expanded saga of the Queen of Sheba is found in the *Kebra Nagast* (*Glory of the Kings*), an Ethiopian text translated from Arabic in 1322. This book describes the history of the country's sovereigns from Solomonic times. The book is understood to be historically accurate by devout Ethiopian Christians; it asserts that the Queen of Sheba was from Ethiopia, her given name was Makeda, and she reigned from 1013 to 982 BCE, according to the Ethiopian calendar. It recounts that Makeda was so captivated by Solomon's learning, she renounced her worship of the sun to follow the God of Israel.

In the *Kebra Nagast*, Solomon desired the queen and wanted to add her to his reputed 400 wives and 600 concubines. He swore he would not take her by force, as long as she did not steal from his house. The queen agreed to this. Solomon then ordered a feast of the spiciest food, which compelled the Queen of Sheba to wake in the night with a great thirst. When she found water to drink, Solomon confronted her and claimed the taking of water was breaking her oath not to steal. Through this trickery, Solomon lured the queen to his bedchamber. Afterwards, he gifted her a ring from his own hand. Makeda took this with her on her return to Ethiopia. On the long journey she gave birth to Solomon's child and named him Menelik, or 'Son of the Wise'.

When Menelik reached the aged of 22, he travelled to Jerusalem to confront his father and proved his identity by displaying the ring Solomon had given his mother. Solomon was delighted to see him and offered him his throne. Menelik turned down the offer of succession and instead returned home with the sons of elders of the kingdom. This entourage secretly smuggled the Ark of the Covenant out of the city and delivered it to Ethiopia (page 168). It's a compelling story, with fairytale elements that are accepted literally by believers. However, what historical evidence of this ancient queen and her court can be traced? Was there a land of Sheba and, if so, was it in Arabia or Africa?

For Ethiopians there is no doubt that the Queen of Sheba was of African origin. It is claimed she returned from Jerusalem by crossing the Red Sea and gave birth to her son in the country of Bâlâ Zadîsârĕyâ (possibly modern-day Eritrea) before reaching her capital at Aksum, today in northern Ethiopia. Aksum, or Axum, was described in the 3rd century CE by the Persian prophet Mani as on a par with Persia, Rome and China. The kingdom controlled an area that encompassed much of modern-day Ethiopia, Eritrea, Djibouti, Sudan and Yemen. The first coinage in sub-Saharan Africa was minted here, and its port of Adulis was key to the trade route between Rome and India. Among its surviving ancient monuments are colossal stelea (slabs) measuring up to 33 m (108 ft) tall. Although Aksum was once a powerful kingdom, archaeological studies have revealed that it was only founded in the 1st century CE , much later than the period of Solomon and Sheba.

Older ruins can be found 50 km (32 miles) east of Aksum, in Yeha. This pre-Aksumite temple, dating from around 700BCE, is the oldest standing structure in Ethiopia. Tombs, possibly belonging to royalty, have been uncovered nearby, along with statues of women and stones bearing inscriptions in the language of the Sabaeans. And it is the Sabaeans we must look to for a more likely origin.

## THE QUEEN OF SABA'?

Saba', a pre-Islamic kingdom in southern Arabia (in present-day Yemen), is a more plausible home for the Queen of Sheba. With its capital Ma'rib or Mayrab, Saba' was well known in the ancient world. Stone inscriptions date the kingdom to at least the 8th century BCE. Archaeological discoveries suggest trade between the Middle East and Saba' took place as far back as 800BCE and that it had a considerable influence on the language, architecture and culture of pre-Aksumite Ethiopia. The Queen of Sheba's visit to Jerusalem could well have been part of a trade mission. In 2012, excavations near Jerusalem's Temple Mount uncovered a 3,000-year-old inscription on a ceramic jar which has been interpreted as being in the Sabaean language. If correct, this may be proof of trade in incense between the Kingdom of Judah and Saba' during the 10th century BCE.

Saba' was a fertile land, thanks to the construction of a vast dam north of Ma'rib during the first millennium BCE. At 680 m (2,200 ft) long and 18 m (59 ft) high, the dam collected enough water to irrigate 100 sq km (30 square miles) of land. A sluice gate and stone walls still remain from this extraordinary example of hydro-engineering, which lasted for seven centuries. The remains of several temples from the 8th century BCE have also been discovered in the region, which are proof of a significant civilization around the proposed time of the Queen of Sheba.

## THE ISLAMIC TRADITION: BILQĪS

In Islamic tradition, the Queen of Sheba is named Bilqīs, or 'the queen of the south', and a sanctuary in Awwan is now named Mahram Bilqīs in her honour (although no inscription at the site mentions her). Instead, the temple is dedicated to Almaqah, the Lord of the Moon. Located outside Ma'rib, probably along a pilgrimage route, the temple has been dated by an inscription from the mid-7th century BCE.

Another temple located nearby, Bar'an, is thought to date from the 8th century BCE. Dubbed the 'Throne of Bilqīs', at its heart is a

Ethiopian depiction of the Queen of Sheba on her way to meet King Solomon.

row of six columns with decorated crowns and a sacred well, with a pool fed by a spout shaped like the head of a bull. Sadly, neither of the Sabaean temples provide any evidence for a Queen of Sheba. What they do reveal, though, is a thriving and wealthy culture that bridged the Red Sea during the era of King Solomon.

Outside of religious texts, there is no evidence for the existence of the Queen of Sheba, or Solomon for that matter, although mentions of other Arab queens do exist. Assyrian records describe tributes from an 8th-century BCE queen named Zabibe, her successors Šamsi and Yaṭi'e, and another queen named Te'elḫunu. A female sovereign, like the Queen of Sheba, was not an anomaly.

Trade missions between southern Arabia and Mesopotamia (broadly, south-east Türkiye, Iraq and eastern Syria) had existed since the early 9th century BCE. The gifts of incense, spices and precious gems that the Queen of Sheba brought to Solomon are likely to have come from the Horn of Africa, Oman or Yemen. Frankincense is still produced from the Boswellia trees in the region. While the Queen of Sheba is not specifically named, these records make the story of a travelling Sabaean queen all the more credible.

The rulers of Aksum converted to Christianity in the 4th century through the influence of Greek-speaking missionaries from Syria and Egypt. Later kings would revive the story of Solomon and Sheba, using the *Kebra Nagast to* make claims of Solomonic ancestry, providing their dynasty with prestige. The last of these emperors, Haile Selassie, had his divine right to rule enshrined in the Ethiopian Constitution of 1955. For the Christians of Ethiopia, the Queen of Sheba was a real person, as well as being the reason for their faith and the mother of their nation.

Whether she was based on a real individual or not, the Queen of Sheba lives on in legend. Such is her allure, she has been portrayed numerous times in medieval poetry. Sculptures of her can be found in the Gothic cathedrals of Amiens, Chartres, Reims and Wells. She is portrayed in stained glass in the cathedrals of Canterbury, Rochester and Strasbourg. She features in Renaissance art, on the bronze doors of the Baptistery in Florence, in frescoes in Pisa and the Vatican, and paintings by Piero della Francesca, Tintoretto and Veronese. Her status has become somewhat clouded, however, by later portrayals of her as an exotic seductress, particularly in films.

Archaeologists may yet find proof of her reign inscribed on a monolith, reasserting her role as a powerful monarch of an Arabian or African nation. Myth or not, the Queen of Sheba has made her mark on history.

# IS THE YONAGUNI MONUMENT AN ANCIENT PYRAMID?

In 1986 Kihachiro Aratake, a director of the Yonaguni-Cho Tourism Association, was diving off the coast of Yonaguni Island, one of the Japanese Ryukyu Islands located off the east coast of Taiwan. The waters were popular with scuba divers because of a large population of hammerhead sharks and manta rays. While he was around 25 m (80 ft) below the surface, Aratake noticed a series of unusual rocky formations on the seabed. They formed a pyramid, with wide ledges or steps that appeared to be clean cut, with chiselled straight edges. At 25 m (80 ft) tall, 100 m (330 ft) long, and 60 m (200 ft) wide, this was a colossal structure that to Aratake's eyes seemed unnatural. Had he accidentally come across the remains of some ancient construction, maybe even a Japanese Atlantis?

Certainly, Aratake's discovery deserved further investigation. Once news of the underwater 'edifice' spread, a promontory on the neighbouring island was unofficially renamed Iseki Hanto (Ruins Point). Several surveys followed, including sonic soundings using underwater robots, conducted by the marine geologist Masaaki Kimura from the University of the Ryukyus, over a 15-year period from 1992. What Kimura recorded convinced him that the structure was human made. He estimated the age of the so-called Yonaguni Monument at 10,000 years, based on the size of stalactites in nearby underwater caves. According to Kimura, the pyramid was the remains of the lost continent of Mu.

## THE LOST CONTINENT OF MU

The story of Mu has many parallels with the legend of Atlantis (page 13). Considered a thriving and advanced society, ancient Mu became submerged following an earthquake or storm. Refugees from this sunken land are said to have spearheaded civilizations in North Africa and Mesoamerica (the historic region spanning areas in southern Mexico and Central America).

Mu was a lost continent first hypothesized by the British-American antiquarian Augustus Le Plongeon in the late 19th century. His studies of Maya ruins in the Yucatán peninsula in Central America, and his translation of their surviving texts, the *Popol Vuh*, led him to believe the Maya were far more ancient than Greek or Egyptian civilizations and originated in a continent called Mu. He took the name 'Mu' from a mistranslation of another pre-Columbian Maya book. Le Plongeon claimed Mu had disappeared underwater following an ancient cataclysmic event.

The publication of Ignatius Donnelly's book *Atlantis: The Antediluvian World* in 1882 led Le Plongeon to identify his Mu with Atlantis. A few decades later, Mu was popularized in a series of books by the British writer James Churchward. He described the continent as stretching from Hawaii to Easter Island in the Pacific Ocean. Churchward's Mu mythology was said to have come directly from a series of translated ancient stone tablets revealed to him by a priest during his early years in India. The tablets were supposed to have originated from Mu and were written in a dead language that only three people could understand. Churchward learned the language and discovered that Mu was a natural paradise that existed between 50,000 and 12,000 years ago. It was home to a people known as the Naacal who used their advanced skills in engineering and agriculture to build sophisticated irrigation systems, magnificent temples and megalithic structures before they were engulfed by a mighty cataclysm around 10,000BCE.

As further evidence, Churchward provided a translation of a pre-Columbian Maya book known as the *Manuscript Troano* or *Codex of Madrid*. This text recounts: 'In the year 6 Kan, on the 11th Mulac in the month Zac, there occurred terrible earthquakes, which continued without interruption until the 13th Chuen. The country of the hills of Mud – the land of Mu – was sacrificed; being twice heaved up it disappeared during one night, the basin being continually shaken by volcanic forces. Being confined, this caused the land to sink and to rise several times and in various places. At last the surface gave away and ten countries were become asunder and scattered; unable to stand the force of the convulsions, Mu sank with 64,000,000 inhabitants.' However, Churchward's work has since been debunked by scientists and is regarded as a hoax.

Modern scientific knowledge about the behaviour of plate tectonics has certainly ruled out the submergence of an early continent such as Mu. Professor Masaaki Kimura himself revised his estimates for the age of the Yonaguni site down to 2,000–3,000 years. He also identified the culture behind it as the less fanciful Yamatai, who lived on the Japanese islands between 1000BCE and 300CE.

As for the submergence of the rocks, the Japanese archipelago is well known for enduring frequent earthquakes and volcanic eruptions. The islands are positioned on a belt of volcanoes that skirt the Pacific Ocean, created over millennia by the collision of tectonic plates. This area of high volcanic and seismic activity is known as the 'Ring of Fire': about 90 per cent of Earth's earthquakes occur here. In 1771, one of the world's largest recorded tsunamis struck Yonaguni Jima (Island) with an estimated height of more than 40 m (131 ft).

What of the site itself? Did it truly resemble a building? In his reports, Kimura described steps, terraces, wall foundations, roads and drainage channels linking the pyramid to castles, a triumphal arch, five temples and a stadium. In all, he identified ten structures covering an area measuring 300 m by 150 m (984 by 492 ft).

## MADE BY HUMANS OR NATURE?

Kimura reported seeing statues of animals (possibly turtles), a large head with eye sockets like the *moai* of Easter Island (page 36), holes where posts could once have fitted, carvings and even a shale tablet etched with symbols resembling a cross and a 'V' shape. 'I think it's very difficult to explain away their origin as being purely natural, because of the vast amount of evidence of man's influence on the structures,' he said at the time. The carvings, according to Kimura, were of Asian origin, with one underwater sphinx resembling a Chinese or ancient Okinawan king. Kimura believed markings in the rocks were made using an ancient cutting tool called a *kusabi*.

Kimura received support for his assumptions from Toru Ouchi, an associate professor of seismology at Kobe University, who also dived the site. Ouchi did not believe the structure could have been caused by tectonic activity. 'What Professor Kimura says is not exaggerated at all. It's easy to tell that those relics were not caused by earthquakes,' he claimed.

The American geologist Robert Schoch, from the University of Boston, also dived the Yonaguni site on several occasions from 1997. He saw it in a completely different light. 'The first time I dived there, I knew it was not artificial,' Schoch said. 'It's not as regular as many people claim, and the right angles and symmetry don't add up in many places. It's basic geology and classic stratigraphy [the study of rock layers] for sandstones, which tend to break along planes and give you these very straight edges, particularly in an area with lots of faults and tectonic activity.'

Had the monument been carved and constructed by humans, Schoch estimated it would be at least 8,000 years old, the last time the area was above water following natural rises and drops in sea level. Schoch pointed out that the structure was not assembled with blocks of stone, but made of sedimentary bedrock, mudstone and sandstone, with visible layers and splits causes by tectonic activity.

A diver explores the mysterious Yonaguni formation off the coast of Japan.

For him, the steps were the result of natural erosion, which would follow these sharp splits. Indeed, many of the steps are so high they could not be walked up without the aid of a ladder. Schoch stated, 'You get a regular blocky structure quite naturally.' In addition, he argued that Kimura's 'roads' were merely channels swept clean by water currents and the 'post holes' were caused by underwater eddies scouring at depressions. Schoch also saw no evidence of human carving, only naturally occurring scratches. Some possible stone tools were found at the site, one of which appeared to be a hand axe or adze. Rather than tools used for carving or scoring the underwater structure, it's likely these were used as farming tools and could easily have fallen into the water.

However, Schoch did not rule out the possibility of some evidence of human modification of the rocks being found in the future, or that the stones had been quarried for building in the distant past. He noted that ancient tombs on Yonaguni Island bear architectural similarities to the underwater site. The builders may have been influenced by the arrangement of rocks off the coast. Schoch also suggested that the formation may have served as a dock for early seafarers.

A topographic study of Yonaguni and neighbouring sites in 2019 by researchers, including Takayuki Ogata, an associate professor from the University of the Ryukyus, provided a clear three-dimensional model of its structure. Their study concluded that while the Yonaguni Monument may look artificial, it was a natural feature formed by weathering and erosion. There are other naturally occurring examples of blocky and geometric structures on Earth, such as Northern Ireland's Giant's Causeway, where interlocking basalt columns were formed through volcanic activity. There are even similar formations north of Yonaguni, such as the stepped rocks at Sanninudai.

The Japanese government has come to its own conclusions. Neither its Agency for Cultural Affairs nor the government of Okinawa Prefecture has chosen to give the underwater site any special protection. The Yonaguni Monument is, therefore, open for divers and researchers to explore at their leisure. While it seems unlikely to be the sunken remains of a town or even a long-lost continent, it remains an evocative dive destination.

# WHAT HAPPENED TO THE PEOPLE OF EASTER ISLAND?

For centuries Rapa Nui was the most remote inhabited island on Earth; it is located around 2,000 km (1,200 miles) from the next inhabited island and over half this distance again from mainland Chile. When European sailors came across this tiny volcanic land mass on Easter Sunday 1722, they named it Easter Island. Fifty years later, when British sailors arrived, they found the population diminished and poorly nourished, and many of their large statues toppled and smashed. What caused the native population of Rapa Nui to almost die out, and what was the significance of their imposing statues?

When Europeans first discovered it, the island was already inhabited by a large population of Polynesian descent, who were eking out a living off the land and surrounding waters. The visitors were astounded by the giant statues erected around the coast, their huge heads and torsos facing inland. The Dutch admiral Jacob Roggeveen, who led the fleet on its brief visit, reported, 'The island is planted with monstrous great statues, the work of I don't know what race, today degenerate or vanished; its great remains an enigma.' In the local language, these gigantic figures were known as the *moai*.

## INCREDIBLE VOYAGES

At only 23 km (14 miles) long and 11 km (7 miles) wide, and with an isolated location in the south-eastern Pacific Ocean, Rapa Nui is a difficult island to locate. Even so, between 800 and 1,200 years ago, sailors from Polynesian islands managed to navigate their way here aboard rafts or canoes.

Traditionally, the island's history begins with Hau Maka, a priest from the Marquesas Islands, around 3,700 km (2,300 miles) away, who had a vision of Rapa Nui and its location. He sent forth scouts to locate it, and they found it just as the priest had described. Faced with a series of intertribal wars, Hau Maka's chief, Hotu Matu'a, chose to follow the route. He gathered his followers aboard double-hulled canoes loaded with food, water, animals and plants, and set off on a voyage. After two months they arrived at Anakena Bay on Rapa Nui, and went on to build permanent settlements across the island.

Alternative origin stories for the people of Rapa Nui were explored in the 20th century by the Norwegian ethnographer Thor Heyerdahl. He believed that the Polynesians came from Peru and that this explained reports of fair-skinned people on Easter Island. Heyerdahl built a balsa raft to prove that a voyage eastward from South America was possible with the most basic of vessels. (The vessel, *Kon-Tiki*, sailed from Peru to the Tuamoto Islands in Polynesia in 1947.) He also claimed that the *moai* bore more similarity to pre-Inca sculptures than to Polynesian designs. Heyerdahl captured the public imagination with his exploits, but his theories on the pedigree of the Easter Islanders were questioned at the time and later discredited by DNA evidence, which proved the original inhabitants were of Polynesian stock.

Ancient Polynesian sailors are credited with great navigational skills, using the stars, the flight paths of birds and sea and wind currents. They migrated from Samoa to the Marquesas, Pitcairn and Hawaii. It is likely they reached Rapa Nui through a series of scouting voyages from somewhere around Mangareva in French Polynesia. Regardless of the route, sailing such a distance was still an incredible feat for the age.

## FORESTS FUEL THE CREATION OF *MOAI*

The triangular island of Rapa Nui is the result of three volcanoes and their flows coming together half a million years ago. It boasts a sub-tropical climate, but lacks the coral reefs and the abundance of sea life that such a climate typically provides. At the time the Polynesians arrived, the island was probably covered with forests of tall palms and a popular nesting site for albatrosses, terns and petrels. Space was cleared by the new arrivals for the planting of taro, bananas, sugar cane and sweet potato brought from South America. Animals that survived the journey to Rapa Nui included the blue-legged Asian chicken and the Polynesian rat, possibly carried as an emergency food source.

Before long, the pioneers began to splinter into rival clans and started carving figures called *moai* ('images') to represent their ancestors. The *moai* were understood to impart a spiritual force known as *mana* – a combination of power and prosperity – to the leaders of each clan. Rivals competed to shape larger and more powerful *moai*. To create them, teams used basalt hand-chisels to quarry and shape compressed volcanic ash, or lapilli tuff, from the slopes of the island's extinct volcano, Rano Raraku.

The *moai* vary in height from 2 m (6.5 ft) to 10 m (33 ft). The largest is 'El Gigante', which lies horizontal in situ in the quarry; it is 21 m (69 ft) long and thought to weigh 200 tonnes. The statues have a simple torso, usually to human-thigh height, although a number are partially buried by shifting soils. Some *moai* wear red stone crowns called *pukao* on their heads and bear eyeballs of white coral and black obsidian.

The impressive number and scale of the statues prompted some later visitors to theorize that extraterrestrial help was needed to

Ahu Ko Te Riku, the only *moai* with a top-knot and eyeballs on Rapa Nui.

construct them. The Swiss author Erich van Däniken, who was noted for his pseudoscientific ideas, suggested aliens may have been stranded on the island and shared their skills. Presumably, he said, this was why the *moai* had such a strange appearance.

Almost 1,000 *moai* were made, but only a quarter were lifted and dragged to their intended positions on stone platforms called *ahu*, usually by the coast. Much effort was spent in the crafting and positioning of these statues. The carving of a single *moai* may have occupied a team of five or six men for a year. As proven by a team led by Thor Heyerdahl in 1955, hundreds could have worked in tandem to drag the *moai*, some weighing 82 tonnes, on tree-cut wooden rollers across the rugged landscape, before days were spent raising each figure on to its plinth. Alternatively, upright *moai* may have been 'walked' to their coastal pedestals by rocking the figure using ropes, a method tested by the Czech engineer Pavel Pavel in 1986.

For an island with limited resources, cutting down trees for rollers and occupying men with major sculpture and relocation exercises may seem wasteful, but the *moai* obviously held great spiritual meaning for the people of Rapa Nui. So, why, around the year 1600, was work on the *moai* halted and why were most of the figures left at the Rano Raraku quarry site?

## DEFORESTATION AND THE DECLINE OF THE *MOAI*

At its height around 1350CE, Rapa Nui may have had a population of up to 15,000. By the 18th century, this population had dropped to between 2,000 and 3,000, sustained by farming crops and breeding domestic chickens. One theory for its decline involves dramatic deforestation: that is, wood was used up for fuel, canoe building and rollers for moving *moai*. The seeds of the trees failed to sprout because they were attacked by the imported Polynesian rats. Without tree roots to hold top soil in place, erosion occurred, reducing the amount of useful agricultural land. Without wood for boats, sea-fishing and migration became less viable. Land birds were eaten to extinction, while sea birds left the island for lack of safe roosts. As the island had suffered serious environmental degradation, people's trust in their ancestors' protection via the *moai* decreased. A new 'Bird Man' cult arose instead.

Described in petroglyphs, or rock carvings, the Bird Man cult involved an annual competition in which men raced to steal the first egg from the migrating sooty tern. The winner became that year's Bird Man and he would then live in isolation, growing his nails long like talons and owning a paddle as a sign of office. The Bird Man would be the new conduit to the dead. Belief in the power of the *moai* decreased and many were toppled in wars between clans. This process was exacerbated by diminishing resources, driven by heavy competition for land, food and water.

This theory of a population depleting its resources through overpopulation and ancestor worship is compelling, not least because it resonates with current global concerns about over-farming, sustainability and climate change. Yet it may not be entirely true.

Archaeological studies suggest that a major societal collapse never actually happened: that the population did not reach the tens of thousands and was in fact increasing at the time the Europeans arrived. Depleted soils could have been revived, using pulverized volcanic rocks that replaced nutrients. There is evidence from pollen counts, however, that show the palm trees, which provided wood, and the mulberry trees used for making rope were gone by around 1500. Without these resources, it would no longer have been possible to transport the *moai* from the quarries.

The English navigator Captain James Cook visited the island in 1774, 50 years after the Dutch discovery. He reported: 'The country appeared barren and without wood; there were, nevertheless, several plantations of potatoes, plantains, and sugar-canes; we also saw some fowls, and found a well of brackish water.' Cook sent a party of men ashore to explore the island. He recorded their findings: 'On the east side, near the sea, they met with three platforms of stone-work, or rather the ruins of them. On each had stood four of those large statues, but they were all fallen down from two of them, and also one from the third; all except one were broken by the fall, or in some measure defaced.'

Cook provided his own observations about the *moai*. 'The gigantic statues, so often mentioned, are not, in my opinion, looked

*Moai* heads on the slopes of Rano Raraku, Rapa Nui.

upon as idols by the present inhabitants… I rather suppose that they are burying-places for certain tribes or families. I, as well as some others, saw a human skeleton lying in one of the platforms, just covered with stones.' Although the *moai* seemed to be neglected, they still impressed the English captain and crew. Cook wrote, 'We could hardly conceive how these islanders, wholly unacquainted with any mechanical power, could raise such stupendous figures, and afterwards place the large cylindric stones before mentioned upon their heads…they must have been a work of immense time, and sufficiently shew the ingenuity and perseverance of these islanders in the age in which they were built; for the present inhabitants have most certainly had no hand in them, as they do not even repair the foundations of those which are going to decay.' Cook also noted that the islanders named each one of the *moai*: names such as Gotomoara, Marapate, Kanaro, Goway-too-goo and Matta Matta were perhaps the titles of deceased chieftains.

## A POPULATION AND CULTURE CLOSE TO DESTRUCTION

The trauma of wood and food shortages and intertribal wars was nothing compared to the calamitous changes brought upon Rapa Nui by European and American arrivals. In 1862, Peruvian slavers began a series of raids on the island, removing around 1,500 men and women – half of the population, including the island's chief and heir – for the slave trade. Ninety per cent of these captives died within two years. The few that were released from bondage and returned to Rapa Nui caught smallpox en route. This caused further devastation among the inhabitants.

Christian missionaries arrived a year later, and began convincing the islanders to give up their ancestor worship and build Christian churches instead. The change in beliefs did not protect the locals from an epidemic of tuberculosis in 1867. A quarter of Rapa Nui's remaining population of 1,200 died. Scottish ranchers began moving on to the lands owned by the deceased, and the local people were herded into fenced villages to make way. By 1877, there were only 111 original Rapa Nui people left on the island – a total far outnumbered by the island's giant statues. Such were their miserable conditions, many islanders chose to relocate to Tahiti to work on plantations. Even though the population on Rapa Nui slowly increased from this low point, much of the history and culture that had been passed down through generations was lost.

Part of the historical legacy lost over the centuries is the written language of the Easter Islanders. A hieroglyphic script called Rongorongo was first recorded by a missionary, Eugène Eyraud, who visited the island in 1864. He found pictograms (carvings on wood) depicting human figures, birds, fish, plants and the sun on wooden tablets and staffs, but failed to get them translated. A year later, most of these wooden records had been destroyed, possibly in a purge by later Christian missionaries or maybe because they were used as fuel as their religious importance diminished. Only 27 objects featuring 120 or so Rongorongo characters now survive, mostly in museums far away from Easter Island. Carbon dating of the wood has proven that the script was used for hundreds of years before Europeans arrived. The messages these symbols represent remain undeciphered, but it has been suggested that the pictograms were used to direct religious chants.

Although the population collapse prior to the arrival of Europeans may be exaggerated, it is clear that degradation of the landscape and some reduction of natural resources did occur on Rapa Nui, and this deterioration probably provoked some inter-clan hostilities. The creation of the *moai* reached a natural end though lack of faith and materials to transport the statues. Several were toppled probably due to the frustrations relating to these shortages, but the islanders were more troubled by the impact of slavery and disease during the 19th century.

Today, the population of Rapa Nui has swelled to about 7,750, an almost even split between those with Polynesian heritage and Chileans. The island has been claimed by the Chilean government for over 130 years. Chile designated the island as a national park in 1935 and it is now a major tourist destination. As with the first European arrivals 300 years ago, visitors are awed and moved by the enigmatic gaze of the *moai*, as representations of strong beliefs, huge communal effort, and resilience in an unforgiving landscape. We can only speculate about the full extent of the trials and turbulent history these silent sentinels have witnessed.

# WAS THERE A MINOAN LABYRINTH?

The idea of a monstrous creature resulting from the coupling between a woman and a bull, under the influence of a disgruntled god, is par for the course in classical Greek mythology, and an idea that can be quickly dismissed as imagined. But did the maze and the court of King Minos, who gave his name to the legendary Minotaur, actually exist? How much of the myth matches archaeological finds, and what is the significance of the bull in Cretan history?

In Greek legend, Asterius the Minotaur was a monster with the body of a man and the head, horns and tail of a bull. He was the offspring of Pasiphaë, wife of King Minos of Crete, and a white bull sent by the god Poseidon. (After Minos failed to sacrifice the bull, an angry Poseidon made his wife fall in love with the creature.) Minos was appalled by his stepson and instructed his architect, Daedalus, to construct an underground labyrinth to house the Minotaur. The Labyrinth was designed so that anyone who should enter it would find it impossible to leave.

The Minotaur was fed with the flesh of seven young men and seven young women sent from Athens as restitution for the murder of King Minos's son Androgeos. Wishing to end the slaughter of these innocents, the Athenian hero Theseus hid among the 14 sacrificial youths. In Crete, Minos's daughter Ariadne promptly fell in love with Theseus and tried to save him from a grim fate in the maze. She provided Theseus with a ball of twine, which he unwound and used to map his way in and out of the maze. In the heart of the Labyrinth Theseus fought and slew the Minotaur. He saved the young Athenians and led them back out the maze, before sailing away from Crete with Ariadne.

## KING MINOS IN HISTORY

Minos was identified as the king of ancient Crete in Homer's epic poem, the *Iliad*, thought to have been written in the late 8th or early 7th century BCE. While Homer does not mention the Minotaur, he does describe a dance floor designed by Daedalus for Ariadne. Perhaps this bore a maze pattern. In the 5th century BCE, Minos was mentioned in the historian Herodotus's *Histories* as a pre-Trojan

Coin from Knossos showing square labyrinth, 350–200 BCE.

War ruler of Crete; yet again, though, there is no mention of the monster in the maze. The Athenian chronicler Thucydides also describes Minos as a historical figure: a conqueror who built the first navy to claim the 30 islands of the Cyclades and cleared the sea of pirates to allow the safe passage of trade across the Aegean.

There appears to be plentiful evidence that a King Minos once existed. Homer was a poet but he weaved entertaining myths around historic settings. Herodotus and Thucydides considered themselves historians rather than storytellers. While their accounts do include inconsistencies and some barely credible descriptions, their reports are considered to be generally reliable.

The 'Minoan' civilization (a term invented in the early 20th century, as at the top of page 49) centred on the island of Crete and incorporated neighbouring islands in the Aegean. It has been linked with the lost island nation of Atlantis (page 13), since it was also a great power long before Hellenic dominance. The island of Thera (now Santorini) was the site of the Minoan settlement Akrotiri, which was buried under ash following a volcanic eruption around 1600BCE. The eruption and a tsunami that followed were said to be the origin of Plato's version of Atlantis.

Knossos, near the north coast of the Mediterranean island of Crete, and the capital of Minos's kingdom, has been associated with the legend of the Minotaur for centuries. Coins minted around 500BCE would occasionally be discovered, bearing an image of a square maze on one side and the Minotaur on the reverse. Archaeologists believed there had to be more evidence from the past lurking underground. In the 19th century, a local Cretan businessman and amateur archaeologist named Minos Kalokairinos was eager to find it. He chose Kephala Hill in northern Crete to begin his search. Sure enough, in 1878 he unearthed the first indication of a Bronze-Age palace complex, storage rooms and the corner of what would later be described as a throne room. Kalokairinos was quick to associate his finds with the legendary King Minos. However, his excavations came to a sudden halt; just three weeks into the dig, he was ordered to stop by the Ottoman Turkish authorities who governed the island at that time. There were concerns that his finds (which included several large *pithoii*, or storage jars) would be shipped to Constantinople (modern-day Istanbul). While unable to pursue his investigations, Kalokairinos shared what he had found thus far, informing museums around Europe and escorting visitors around the site. One visitor was the British archaeologist Sir Arthur Evans.

When Crete gained its independence in 1898, Evans launched his bid the excavate the Knossos site himself, by buying the land and getting a permit. He began his excavations in 1900, without the involvement of Kalokairinos. Also interpreting the site as the palace of King Minos, it was Evans who chose the name 'Minoan' to describe the civilization that built it.

## A VAST PALACE AT KNOSSOS

Evans' excavations slowly revealed a vast complex of a thousand or so rooms and compartments spread over several storeys. However, the buildings he uncovered may not be a royal residence, as first thought. They could have been used for religious and administrative purposes and may have housed an elite, rather than a sole ruler.

There are two constructions on the site, the first dating from around 2000–1700BCE. In style, this matches contemporary Cretan complexes in Malia and Phaestos, with walls and flooring painted with red ochre. They may have been destroyed through some natural disaster, such as an earthquake. A second, grander building was erected on the ruins and dates from between 1700BCE and 1490BCE. This seems to have been built in the same period as several other complexes, including those at Zakros and Petras.

Knossos was the largest of all the Minoan complexes found on Crete. The building lacks fortifications, which suggests a generally peaceful period of rule, although some swords, daggers and arrowheads have been unearthed. The complex rises around a central court and encompasses 2.4 hectares (6 acres). Two floors are linked by a colossal staircase. The ground floor includes 16 store rooms for jars of oil, wine and grain, and a space identified by Evans as a throne room, complete with alabaster seating and benches made of gypsum flanked by frescoes of griffins. Two dark rooms are presumed to have been used for religious rituals. The upper level houses rooms of state. The complex also features bathrooms and a sophisticated drainage system. Outside is a theatre with the capacity for 400 spectators.

Knossos was part of a wide-reaching civilization for at least five centuries. It appears to have successfully traded in oil, wine and wool, as well as highly decorated pottery which has been unearthed in Egypt, Syria, Anatolia, Sicily and mainland Greece.

During his excavations, Sir Arthur Evans took some liberties, reconstructing parts of the palace and repainting frescoes when the originals were removed for museums. He also turned the site into a major tourist attraction. Among the site's treasures were many clay tablets inscribed with Linear A and Linear B; these scripts were used by the Minoan and Mycenaean cultures, the latter developing into the Greek alphabet. The text, as deciphered 50 years after Evans' discovery (and his death in 1941), shares details of trade

Part-reconstructed palace at Knossos, Crete, with fresco of a bull.

in flax, textiles and oils, along with the distribution of rations and mention of Greek deities.

There were also images of bulls on frescoes and pottery sherds. These depict athletic youths leaping over the backs of the beasts. There are several limestone horn-shaped decorations, numerous ritual vessels (called *rhytons*) shaped to resemble a bull's head, and signet rings. These suggest the animal played an important role in Minoan customs. Could this culture have venerated the bull in some way and inspired the tale of the Minotaur in the maze?

Another recurring image within the palace complex is that of a double axe. The ancient name for this symbol is said to be *labrys*. Evans extrapolated from this and decided that the word 'labyrinth' meant 'House of the double axes' – hence the complex itself, and not an underground maze, was the Labyrinth.

One could imagine getting lost in the thousand rooms of this four-storey complex. Is it far-fetched to describe it as labyrinthine? Labyrinths certainly existed before this famous example. Herodotus described one at Crocodilopolis, south of Cairo in Egypt: that partly subterranean example supposedly featured 3,000 chambers.

It may be that the tale of the hero Theseus freeing Athens from its blood debt to Crete represented the ending of Minoan dominance over Greece. By 1420BCE, the Minoans were under the thumb of the Mycenaean civilization, which assumed control by force or assimilation. The buildings at Knossos were destroyed by fire around 1350BCE and the site largely abandoned around 1200BCE.

Under Roman rule from 69BCE, Knossos was displaced as the capital of Crete by Gortyn, a city 60 km (37 miles) further south. Building Gortyn required extensive quarrying of a nearby hillside. In the following centuries, the tunnels left behind during this construction work were mistaken for the legendary Labyrinth by various authors.

## 'THE ROOM OF THE CHILDREN'S BONES'

While the tale of the Minotaur may have been inspired by political events, a dark discovery may account for the inclusion of sacrificed youth in the legend. In 1979, Peter Warren, a professor of classical archaeology at Bristol University in the UK, was excavating basement rooms at the palace of Knossos. Among the debris of looms, tools and pottery, he also found one large jar containing the remains of snails and shellfish, plus three human bones with visible cut marks.

Adjacent to this find was 'The Room of the Children's Bones', a store including 251 animal bones belonging to sheep, cattle, pigs and dogs – plus 371 human bones and fragments from at least four children. These also showed signs of cutting with a blade in order to remove flesh. Were children being served along with animal flesh, or were these ghastly remains leftovers from some cult practice?

Some experts believe the sacrifice of children was the action of desperate priests trying to ward off earthquakes, which were common on the island. Remains at a number of sites on Crete support this theory. One find at Anemospilia, 32 km (20 miles) from Knossos, comprised three adults, one carrying a ceremonial vase, beside the body of a young man who had possibly been tied up, and placed on an altar-like platform next to a bronze dagger. This proposed bloody attempt to thwart earthquakes failed, as the quartet were crushed when the walls and roof of their chamber collapsed following a tremor.

There seems to be enough evidence to confirm that some child sacrifice took place in Bronze-Age Crete. This could have inspired the account of seven male and seven female Athenians being brought to the island as offerings to the Minotaur. Alternatively, it may have arisen from instances of actual sacrifice by a bull-worshipping cult.

One interesting theory on the identity of the Minotaur suggests that the bull was an early Cretan representation of a sun-god – a creature symbolizing power and fertility – and that King Minos and the Minotaur were the same revered being. Minos's wife Pasiphaë's union with a bull may then have been ceremonial.

The Minoan civilization, or whatever this culture called itself, has long been associated with the story of the bull-man in the Labyrinth. While the tale may be regarded as legendary, and the hybrid monster a fantasy, the existence of a Labyrinth on Crete and a tribute in flesh may not be so far-fetched. Like Ariadne's twine, the discoveries at Knossos may yet provide a thread that leads us out of the darkness.

# WHAT CAUSED THE COLLAPSE OF THE HARAPPAN CIVILIZATION?

In the 19th century a chance find would lead to the discovery of a lost civilization in a region of northern India that revolutionized South Asian history. The Harappan Civilization, as it is now known, is thought to be a thousand years older than any previously discovered culture in India. Later study revealed it to have been a sophisticated and vast urban empire. How did one of the world's earliest urban civilizations come to exist, and why did it disintegrate?

## AN OPPORTUNIST FINDS A CLUE

In 1827, Private James Lewis deserted his British East India Company army post. He fled the company's base in Agra, northern India, and took on a new identity as Charles Masson. Claiming to be a scholar and a doctor, Masson set out across the Thar Desert. He managed to evade army justice for years, crossing Afghanistan, where he was beaten and robbed more than once. In the Persian Gulf he convinced British officers that he was an American traveller with knowledge of a lost Alexandrian tomb in the Punjab (modern-day eastern Pakistan and north-western India). Masson was fascinated with the ancient histories of Alexander the Great and could weave a good yarn. With funding from Britain's envoy to Persia, Masson followed what he understood to be the campaign route of Alexander's armies.

In 326BCE, after years of successful conquests that expanded the Macedonian Empire, Alexander the Great's exhausted and homesick armies paused while campaigning in India. Alexander's envoy, Aristoboulos, surveyed the valley and the lower reaches of the Indus River. He found it abandoned and thousands of villages unoccupied, following the redirection of the river. Soon after, Alexander's army would turn back towards home. On his own campaign, 2,000 years later, Masson hoped to find evidence, at the very least, of Alexandrian army camps. He actually discovered much more, but failed to realize the significance of what he had stumbled across.

After a long trek through thick undergrowth, Masson came across an artificial mound near the village of Harappa, south-west of Lahore. Masson wrote of his travels in 1842: 'East of the village was an abundance of luxuriant grass, where, along with many others, I went to allow my nag to graze. When I joined the camp I found it in front of the village and ruinous brick castle. Behind us was a large circular mound, or eminence, and to the west was an irregular rocky height, crowned with remains of buildings, in fragments of walls, with niches, after the eastern manner. I examined the remains on the height, and found two circular perforated stones, affirmed to have been used as bangles, or arm-rings, by a faquir of renown. The walls and towers of the castle are remarkably high, though, from having been long deserted, they exhibit in some parts the ravages of time and decay.' Masson assumed this was Sangala, a city razed by Alexander the Great's troops in 326BCE. Unfortunately, Masson's sketch of the site was lost, and his report of the ruins was never followed up.

Later, in 1856, while constructing the railway from Multan to Lahore, the engineer William Brunton came across materials that he thought would make ideal ballast for the tracks at the same village of Harappa. Thousands of matching bricks were being dug from mounds by locals for their own projects. Such was their uniformity, Brunton assumed that the bricks had only been recently made, and helped himself. Eventually, bricks seized from the site would support more than 100 miles of track, and much of what Masson had seen and sketched was removed.

## AN ANCIENT EMPIRE CHANGES HISTORY

When serious excavations finally took place in 1861, under Alexander Cunningham, director-general of the Archaeological

Survey of India, and later under his successor, John Marshall, these humble bricks led not only to the discovery of a Bronze-Age civilization, but also to the assumed dates of early Indian civilization being pushed back thousands of years.

The civilization that was unearthed proved to be on the scale of ancient Egypt, with a population in the millions and trading relationships with Mesopotamia (an ancient region forming part of today's Iraq) and Central Asia. A lost culture had been found but, after decades of archaeology and study, much remains unknown about this far-reaching society. Its language is undeciphered and the reasons for its demise remain a subject of debate. Who were the Harappans, and why did their culture turn to ruin?

Among the bricks and rubble that remained after the railway work, Alexander Cunningham's team discovered a small black soapstone seal featuring the image of a bull, plus six characters or hieroglyphs matching no known Indian language. Similar seals included the images of rhinoceroses, elephants and oxen. One humpless beast bore a single curved horn. At first this was interpreted as a unicorn, but now it is understood to be a bull in profile.

Excavations at a second site named Mohenjo-daro ('Mound of the Dead Men'), located 400 km (250 miles) to the south in what is now the Pakistani province of Sindh, revealed remarkable similarities. Over 1,000 further sites have been uncovered from the same period, situated further east along the Yamuna River and westwards into Afghanistan. This Bronze-Age culture, first dubbed the Indus Valley Civilization, soon demanded a new name because it stretched far beyond the Indus River to encompass an area greater than the contemporary empire of Mesopotamia. It is now known as the Harappan Civilization, after the site of its first discovery, and has been dated to 3300–

1300BCE, a millennium earlier than any previously discovered Indian civilization.

DNA evidence has since traced the origins of the Harappan Civilization to a small village in Pakistan. Excavations at Mehrgarh on the Kachi Plain have revealed the first signs of agriculture in the Indian subcontinent, from around 6500BCE, with the cultivation of barley and domestication of cattle, along with later ceramic production and the use of cotton in clothing. Mehrgarh stretched for almost 300 hectares (750 acres) along the Bolan river and was occupied continuously for an impressive 4,000 years.

## EARLY TOWN PLANNING

Of the Bronze Age sites found, Harappa, Mohenjo-daro and Dholavira all cover more than 100 hectares (247 acres) of land. The settlements follow similar patterns, being built around a grid system directed towards cardinal (compass) points, with regimented road widths. Buildings are in brick, above stone foundations. Unlike other civilizations of the period, there are no ostentatious palaces, religious buildings or major tombs, and no statues or inscriptions suggesting a hierarchy. The cities were arranged with a citadel of civic buildings to the west and a residential quarter to the east. The largest structures were possibly used as granaries and there are communal bitumen-sealed baths. Many homes include bathrooms with sophisticated drainage systems, suggesting an early concern with cleanliness that continues in Hindu rituals today. Some buildings featured 'wind-catchers': roof attachments that provided simple air conditioning. While there is no evidence of royalty, there was clearly an administration in place that regulated building and trade, with standardized weights and measures used across the region. There are cemeteries catering for an elite, containing bodies buried with ornaments and pottery, but little to denote great wealth or status.

Five thousand years ago, the Indus and Ghaggar-Hakra rivers would have served the Harappans well, with a regular delivery of silt from the Tibetan plateau to the Indian floodplains. The remains of a brick flood barrier can be found 6 km (4 miles) to the east of Mohenjo-daro, which was built to divert the Indus from the city. This fertile land would have provided food for large populations, with crops including wheat, barley, pulses and millet. Estimates for the population of Harappa and Mohenjo-daro vary between 30,000 and 60,000 individuals; the entire Harappan Civilization totalled between one and five million people. These people used the wheel, both on ox-pulled carts and for turning pottery. They also designed flat-bottomed sailboats to navigate the shallow river waters and trade abroad.

## A PEACE-LOVING, TRADING CULTURE?

While fortifications were added during the later period of the Harappan Civilization, there is little evidence of warfare and negligible remains of weapons. This suggests the culture enjoyed a fairly peaceful existence.

A number of female figurines, particularly pregnant statuettes, found during excavation hint that some form of fertility ritual took place. The people of the Harappan Civilization may have worshipped a mother goddess. One particularly fine discovery unearthed at Mohenjo-daro is a lithe young woman cast in bronze. This so-called 'dancing girl' is 10 cm (4 in) tall and poses with a hand on her hip and her head raised in a proud manner. She

Excavations at Mohenjo-daro, Sindh, Pakistan.

wears little except several arm bracelets. Another statue, carved in soapstone and smaller in size, is that of a bearded man wearing a headdress and decorative armband. He has been described as a priest-king.

Other finds at the sites included toys, whistles, clay statuettes of cows, bears, monkeys and dogs, and thousands more square stamped seals. From many of the seals, a language involving around 425 symbols was deduced. The language – which does not appear on walls, tombs or statues, only on pottery, tablets and, in most cases, the seals – has never been deciphered, despite the efforts of numerous scholars and computer programmers.

The postage-stamp-sized seals feature between five and 34 characters and the text is understood to run from right to left. Was each symbol a word or syllable? Did the seal bear the name of its owner or a message? Maybe these small items were carried as charms. The symbols bear no relation to any other language, although current thought suggests they may be related to Dravidian languages that predate Sanskrit and are spoken in South India and parts of Afghanistan.

Such seals have been found as far and wide as Oman, Iraq and Central Asia. There is evidence that the Harappans traded copper, gold, tin and ivory with Mesopotamia. Clearly the Harappan Civilization was a major player across the region, equal to Egypt and Mesopotamia in population and reach. So, how did it come to be forgotten?

## THE DECLINE OF THE HARAPPANS

Early theories on the end of the Harappan Civilization pointed the finger at the arrival of a race from Central Asia calling themselves Arya. These paler-skinned nomadic pastoralists, who we now call the Aryans, had domesticated the horse and used it to pull chariots. They wielded bronze weapons and spoke a language that is at the root of many Indo-European languages. The Aryans purportedly drove the people of Harappa southward from their settlements. This invasion theory was enthusiastically supported by Westerners who questioned the notion that Indian civilization could have risen from within.

An Aryan invasion was described in the *Vedas*: religious texts composed in Sanskrit between 1500 and 1200BCE. The *Vedas* were shared orally between Brahmin priests for centuries, before being transcribed around the 6th century BCE, and form the basis of Hinduism. Among their hymns and sacred poetry are passages that describe a wave of chariot-riding warriors who were inspired by the god Indra to wipe out the Harappans.

While the Aryans did become dominant in the north, there is no archaeological evidence of warfare between them and the Harappans. Indeed, there is a two-century gap between the end of the Harappan Civilization and the arrival of the Aryans. It seems the Harappans were giving up on their cities long before the Aryans moved in, and that there was more than one migratory wave. It's likely that the Aryans intermarried with the indigenous population and adopted some of its culture and inventions.

Instead of expulsion, environmental change seems to have been the driving force for the decline of the Harappans. It's thought that a major drought and cooling period took place about 4,200 years ago, which could have weakened the monsoon and the flow of the Ghaggar-Hakra river system. Without water and the silt it supplied, agriculture would have suffered. Excavations show evidence of several major floods at Mohenjo-daro between 1900 and 1700BCE, which caused soil salination. The gathering of wood for the kilns that fired the countless bricks needed for construction resulted in deforestation. Climate change led to tributaries of the Indus finding new channels or drying up completely.

After its peak between 2600 and 1900BCE, the Harappan Civilization declined. Buildings were poorly constructed and maintained, long-distance trade decreased, drains were blocked and bodies were left unburied. Disease thrives in concentrated urban communities; signs of leprosy and tuberculosis have been identified in skeletal remains found in the area. Seals and written language fell out of use as administrative rule declined. Eventually, the large settlements were abandoned. People moved away from the cities and towns to work on rural farms along the Ganges and Yamuna rivers.

Eventually, the Harappan cities and villages were buried in sand and silt. Their crumbling structures were built upon or ransacked for materials until 3,000 years later a tiny seal and an indecipherable code opened a window into a sophisticated and widespread society that turned South Asian history on its head. The quest to understand the Harappan language continues along with excavations. Perhaps one day this lost civilization will be able to tell its own story.

# WHO BUILT GREAT ZIMBABWE?

Hidden from western eyes, in the hinterlands of southern Africa are the remains of a once-mighty kingdom, made wealthy from trade in gold and cattle. When European explorers found the site in the 19th century they linked it with Ophir, the legendary source of King Solomon's wealth. Its local name, Great Zimbabwe, would be adopted by a nation, but what was its true origin? Who built this complex, and where did its people go?

## THE BIBLICAL GOLD-RICH CITY OF OPHIR

Throughout the 19th century much of Africa was carved up by European powers, exploiting the continent's people, produce and minerals. While foreign powers based themselves in trading posts around the coast, they barely explored the interior of the continent due to the risk of contracting tropical diseases like malaria, and fear of attacks from the indigenous people. An intrepid few did venture within, hoping to map the lands and claim riches for their country. Karl Mauch, a German geographer, was one such adventurer. Inspired by biblical legends, he set out to find the fabled city of Ophir, the source of King Solomon's gold. He found both gold and the remains of an ancient city, surrounded by drystone walls and with a mysterious conical tower at its heart. The city had been abandoned to nature only decades earlier. Was this the Ophir that Mauch dreamt of or the African home of the Queen of Sheba (page 23)?

Karl Mauch had been obsessed with Africa since his schooldays in Ludwigsburg, Germany; he studied the continent's flora and directed his energies towards one day filling in the blanks on the African map. After persuading a map publisher to back him, he set sail for southern Africa in 1865. Mauch travelled by foot and ox-cart across the Transvaal, surveying the land and keeping detailed geological notes in his journals. His map of the Transvaal was not a commercial success, but he continued his expeditions and in 1867 he ventured into Mashonaland (in modern north-eastern Zimbabwe) with the elephant hunter Henry Hartley. There, Mauch confirmed the presence of veins of gold along the banks of the Tati River. This discovery triggered a gold rush in southern Africa. Mauch was not the first to find the gold seams, however. They had been mined by natives for perhaps hundreds of years, and supported the rise of an African empire. It was the capital of this ancient empire that Mauch would proceed to discover.

Rather than remain to exploit the gold fields, Mauch continued his mapping activities, passing through areas beset by drought, where people were suffering starvation. One of his early travel companions died of fever in 1870. A year later, following rumours of a great ruin north of the Limpopo river, in Banyailand, Mauch set out to locate what he believed may be evidence of the city of Ophir.

Ophir was identified in the Bible as a source of King Solomon's great wealth – a place where gold, precious stones and 'algum' wood, as well as ivory, monkeys and peacocks, could be found. It was first thought to be located in Arabia, although the 1st-century Jewish historian Josephus preferred India, which was a known habitat for peacocks. Reports of ancient Egyptian trade in similar exotic goods with Punt (Somaliland) also led some to propose eastern Africa. In his epic poem *Paradise Lost*, the English poet John Milton placed the city in central Africa, writing 'And Sofala, thought Ophir, to the realm of Congo, and Angola farthest south…'.

## THE ARRIVAL OF PORTUGUESE TRADERS

From the 10th century, East Africa was a centre of gold trafficking. Swahili traders used river-going dhows to navigate between Sofala, on the coast of Mozambique, and gold mines in the interior. The trade continued into the 15th century, by which time it was also supplying the market for enslaved people. The gold trade caught the attention of the Portuguese, with the historian Thomé Lopes identifying the thriving market with the legendary Ophir.

By 1505, the Portuguese had erected a fort at Sofala and they would build another soon after on Mozambique Island; however, the gold trade was already in decline by this point. Reports had claimed 4,000 tonnes of gold passed through the port every year, but over the first 15 months of the Portuguese presence just 2.6 kg (5.7 lb) was shipped from Sofala. More intrepid Portuguese explorers began venturing inland. In 1506, in a letter to the King of Portugal, the explorer Diogo de Alcáçova wrote of Zunbanhy, the capital of the Kingdom of Mutapa, 'the houses of the king... were of stone and clay, very large and on one level'.

In 1552, the Portuguese historian João de Barros provided reports of gold and a ruined city in southern Africa, including: 'There are other mines in a district called Toroa, which by another name is known as the kingdom of Butua, which is ruled by a prince called Burrom...and these mines are the most ancient known in the country, and they are all in the plain, in the midst of which there is a square fortress, masonry within and without, built of stones of marvellous size, and there appears to be no mortar joining them. This edifice is almost surrounded by hills, upon which are others resembling it in the fashioning of the stone and the absence of mortar, and one of them is a tower more than twelve fathoms high.

'The natives of the country call all these edifices Symbaoe... they say they are the work of the devil, for in comparison with their power and knowledge it does not seem possible to them that they should be the work of man.'

In 1597, the Portuguese Dominican missionary João dos Santos wrote, 'some fragments of old walls and ancient ruins of stone and mortar are still standing...these houses were anciently a factory of the Queen of Sheba, and that from this place a great quantity of gold was brought to her. Others say these are the ruins of the factory of Solomon...the region of Ophir, whence gold was brought to Jerusalem.'

## MAUCH FINDS GREAT ZIMBABWE

Karl Mauch may not have been aware of these centuries-old reports, but he gathered as much information as he could on the lost city's location. He set his sights on the land between the Limpopo and Zambezi rivers and ventured out on 3 July 1871, supported by numerous porters, with whom he had many disagreements. Mauch wore an all-leather outfit designed for the adventure, as protection against thorn bushes and biting insects, but it was heavy and worsened the effects of the heat.

After being deserted by his porters and left alone to defend his supplies for a night, Mauch was escorted by seven young natives to the *kraal* (village) of a local chief named Mapansule, who seemed to covet him as a prize. From here, he was rescued by a German hunter named Adam Renders. Renders was familiar with the ruins that Mauch sought and took him to a safer village within walking distance. The natives of this village feared the site and spoke of 'a pot that hid itself in clefts and bushes on a mountain and at times was changing its position on its own'. Despite this ghost story, Mauch and Renders made their way to the ruins, near modern-day Masvingo in south-central Zimbabwe, on 11 September 1871.

The site was named *Dzimba dzemabwe*, meaning 'Houses of stone', by the Shona, the Bantu-speaking people of the area. This would be translated as 'Great Zimbabwe'. The plot was divided in two main parts: a hill complex and a walled enclosure below, connected by buildings that were too obscured by overgrown vegetation for Mauch to interpret. On the hill, large, curved walls had been built between large boulders to form an oval compound. The walls were formed of cut granite blocks, without mortar to fix them in position.

The complex below, now known as the Great Enclosure, had a wall 244 m (800 ft) in length, and up to 5 m (16 ft) thick, reaching a height of 10 m (33 ft) in places. The top was decorated with a pattern of chevrons. An estimated one million stone blocks were used in its construction. A parallel wall inside created a corridor that was 55 m (180 ft) long. Within this were tall trees, creepers and heaps of

The Great Enclosure's mysterious solid tower.

masonry, plus a curious solid tower that was 9 m (30 ft) high. The purpose of the Great Enclosure was, and remains, unknown. It may have been used as a royal palace or for initiation rites. The tower has no obvious function, except as a symbol of status.

While Mauch was not the first European to see Great Zimbabwe, it was his records and fine drawings that brought it to wider attention. In an attitude that was typical of the time, Mauch could not imagine this edifice to have been built by Africans. He was convinced that it was somehow linked to the Queen of Sheba. This idea was supported by a local name for the Great Enclosure: *Mumbu guru* or 'The House of the Great Woman'. Mauch also mistakenly identified the wood used in beams as cedar from the Lebanon and thought that it must have been transported by Phoenician traders. He deduced, like the Portuguese before him, that the fabled Ophir was the port of Sofala.

Mauch left the site, never to return, and missed the discovery, eight years later, of four birds carved in soapstone. The birds were hidden within a wall of a cattle pen. These treasures were removed, along with pottery sherds, arrowheads and tools, during a survey in 1890 by British archaeologist James Theodore Bent, a member of the Royal Geographical Society. Bent and his team cleared much of the Great Enclosure in order to take photographs and provide detailed plans. He rejected suggestions the site was part of the legend of Solomon and Sheba, concluding that 'the ruins and the things in them are not in any way connected with any known African race'.

A decade later, Richard Nicklin Hall, a British journalist and the so-called 'Curator of Great Zimbabwe', arrived with an agenda to remove any traces of African heritage at the site. His destructive digs uncovered artefacts that matched objects still in use in local villages. Hall rejected these as 'native rubbish' and he continued digging until he discovered gold – according to his claims, an amount worth more than £4,000 (about £600,000 in today's money).

## A CLEARER ASSESSMENT OF GREAT ZIMBABWE

Finally, in 1906, David Randall-MacIver, a British archaeologist who had studied under the renowned British Egyptologist Sir Flinders Petrie, was given permission to excavate the site. His view on the site was untainted by prejudice against Africans. His deep excavations unearthed pottery that clearly matched modern work by the local Makalanga (Shona) people. Randall-MacIver believed that Great Zimbabwe was a distribution centre for gold found in the interior. He judged that it was African built, and dated the enclosure to the 14th or 15th century. His conclusions were rejected by European settlers, who could not accept it was built by natives. Later archaeologists who shared and confirmed Randall-MacIver's verdict faced censorship or imprisonment under the white-minority Rhodesian Front party that governed Rhodesia (now Zimbabwe) in the 1970s.

We now understand that Great Zimbabwe was a major hub for the Shona people, and that it was constructed by their ancestors sometime between 1275 and 1550, based on radiocarbon dating. It was the oldest and the largest of 200 or so walled closures, or *zimbabwe*, and was perfectly positioned between the gold mines of the north and the ports of the Indian Ocean. As such, it prospered through trade in gold, along with ivory and cattle (particularly beef). The plateau site of Great Zimbabwe put it generally out of reach of the tsetse fly, so it was ideal for breeding livestock.

Taking into account all the ruins and mud-brick buildings (*daga*) that surround the hill complex and the walled enclosure, Great Zimbabwe can be considered a city. It covered 7 sq km (2.8 square miles) and could potentially have housed between 11,000 and 18,000 people. The discovery of a glazed Persian bowl, dishes and stoneware from China, and Syrian glass attest to far-reaching trade links during the 13th and 14th centuries.

By around 1700, Great Zimbabwe was empty. The mines and rivers were no longer supplying nuggets of gold. Trade moved away. The environment could no longer sustain a population of thousands as it suffered from over-farming and over-grazing by cattle. Even today, there are some species of tree that will not grow here. Following independence in 1980, Rhodesia took the name Zimbabwe in recognition of this heritage, with one of the soapstone birds being adopted as an emblem of the country. While much mystery still surrounds its form and purpose, Great Zimbabwe is evidence of a major medieval African empire, of a once-wealthy trading civilization.

# WHO LIVED IN THE TUNNELS OF DERINKUYU?

The valleys of Cappadocia draw millions of visitors to Türkiye every year. For most it is an opportunity to hike or take a balloon ride over the area's tooth-like rock formations (the 'fairy chimneys') and visit the cave homes carved into these spires. However, 85 m (280 ft) below ground there exists another world – a maze of tunnels and rooms that were in use for thousands of years. This is the ancient city of Elengubu, known as Malakopia (meaning 'soft') to the last Greek inhabitants, and today known as Derinkuyu. This subterrestrial city had been forgotten for decades, with little known of its history. Rediscovered in the late 20th century, Derinkuyu's winding passageways provided a window on an ancient way of life. Why did so many people in the past choose to hide away from the sun? What did they fear and how did they survive underground?

Derinkuyu is said to be the largest subterranean city on Earth, capable of housing 20,000 dwellers within its 18 levels of tunnels. What has been excavated so far may not even be the full extent of this incredible underworld. Over two millennia, it was the home to Phrygians, Persians, Christians and Greeks.

*Derin kuyu* is Turkish for 'deep well'. For years, Turkish locals drew water from the wells here without knowing anything of the civilization that excavated them. The story goes that Derinkuyu was rediscovered in 1963 thanks to the rather mundane intervention of chickens. While renovating his home, an unnamed Turkish local accidentally caused a small crack in his wall. His chickens used this as an escape route and were never seen again. The owner widened the hole and discovered a long passageway behind it. This was the first of several entrances that opened up from private homes in the area.

When news of the underground passageways broke out, official excavations began and uncovered a lengthy series of tunnels leading to dwellings, food storage areas, wineries, cattle stables, schools and even a chapel. How long had these facilities existed and who had actually dug them out?

## AN ANCIENT UNDERGROUND EXISTENCE

The earliest record of an underground city here dates back to around 370BCE. In his work *Anabasis*, the ancient Greek soldier Xenophon, a student of Socrates, described Anatolian people from the region of Cappadocia who chose not to live in the cliffside caves and instead had burrowed below ground. He wrote, 'The houses here were underground, with a mouth like that of a well, but spacious below; and while entrances were tunnelled down for the beasts of burden, the human inhabitants descended by a ladder. In the houses were goats, sheep, cattle, fowls and their young; and all the animals were reared and took their fodder there in the houses.'

Digging a network of dwellings in Cappadocia is not quite the challenge it might appear. There is little water in the area and the rock is tuff, made from compacted volcano ash. It is soft and easy to cut into with shovels or pickaxes. (The same rock was quarried on Easter Island for the production of the *moai* or giant statues described on page 36.)

Experts believe the first people to have attempted to tunnel in Cappadocia used stone to cut into the rock. These earliest of excavators were likely followed by the Hittites, who carved out usable accommodation, working the rocks with metal tools. The Hittites ruled this part of Anatolia, now Türkiye, from about 1600–1200BCE. As the Hittite Empire collapsed, the Phrygians took over the region. They may have dug out the next level of tunnels between 1200 and 800BCE. The Phrygians' skills in carving monuments in rock is well known. They left their mark in natural rock outcrops, shaping them into shrines and figures, with one notable façade at Türkiye's Midas Kenti (Midas City).

## REFUGES FROM ATTACK AND INVASION

The underground caves were probably used initially as storage facilities but, in the face of numerous invasions, they would have provided a useful haven. In 17CE the arrival of the Romans under Emperor Tiberius may have driven early Christian colonies to seek shelter in the tunnels and to avoid persecution.

The underground city of Derinkuyu, Türkiye.

When the predominantly Christian Byzantine Empire came under attack from Islamic armies from 780CE to 1180CE, the underground population of Derinkuyu and surrounds swelled to possibly 20,000 inhabitants. These Christian natives re-emerged once the Byzantine Empire reasserted control in the 10th century, and began carving their churches into the cliffs above ground at Goreme and Sogamli. These places of worship, and their wall paintings, were left untouched during the later Seljuk and Ottoman eras and are a tourist attraction today. In the 14th century, Derinkuyu was used as a hideout for Christians once more during incursions by the Mongolian armies of Timur (Tamerlane).

Had the tunnels been discovered, they could have been defended easily. The passageways are tight in places, sometimes requiring visitors to stoop. Invaders would have had to enter one by one. Half-tonne boulders were used to block the entrance into each level. These featured peepholes just large enough to jab a spear through. There are also holes in some ceilings that could have been used to repel intruders below. Wells and air ducts were carefully placed and duplicated, limiting the attackers' opportunities to poison the water supply or block it.

## DESIGNED FOR LIVING

At 445 sq km (172 square miles), Derinkuyu is the largest of the 200 known underground complexes beneath the Anatolian Plains. Many are joined by tunnels. Derinkuyu is connected to another large series of caves at Kaymakli by a tunnel that is 9 km (5.6 miles) long and wide enough to allow three people to walk abreast.

Living quarters, schools, meeting places and stables were cut into the higher levels. In the residential rooms, chairs, tables and

Round stones were used to block entrances to different levels in the underground city.

beds are all carved from the rock. One notable benefit of living in the tunnels is that they remain dry and at a comfortable and steady temperature of about 13°C (55°F). Inhabitants would have used sealable clay jars for personal waste, which would be disposed of through tunnels or outside. Exterior entrances and escape routes were hidden behind foliage.

Storage rooms were further below ground, with stairs or foot and hand holes between the levels. There are areas for the production of wine, with vats for pressing grapes and *amphorae* used for storage. On the lowest levels were churches and cells for monks. These were rarely decorated. One of the most notable rooms in the subterranean complex is a large barrel-vaulted chamber which is thought to have been used for religious studies.

Clean water was saved in wells as deep as 55 m (180 ft), enough for the population to survive a lengthy siege. More than 50 air shafts were hacked out to provide fresh air and remove the smoke from torch lights and kitchen fires. The spaces were probably temporary refuges, rather than permanent homes. Some of the passageways can only be crawled through and a life without sunlight would have been intolerable, but they functioned well as makeshift homes and sanctuaries for many waves of refugees.

After 2,000 years of occupation, the tunnels of Derinkuyu were abandoned in 1923, when the Cappadocian Greeks left for Greece as part of a compulsory population exchange with Türkiye, under an internationally ratified agreement.

## MODERN-DAY TOURIST ATTRACTIONS

Since 1969, much of the site has been opened to tourists, although some routes are blocked off for safety reasons and many are still being excavated. The site was awarded Unesco World Heritage status in 1985. In 2014, some space in the city was given purpose again, being rented as a warehouse for fruit and vegetables brought from Türkiye's Mediterranean coast for storing before export.

While the full extent of the underground sanctuary at Derinkuyu is still to be realized, another underground complex at Nevşehir in central Türkiye was discovered in 2013, with a similar number of levels for living spaces, chapels, water channels and air shafts, plus linseed presses for producing oil for lamps to light the passageways. Surveys by geophysicists from Nevşehir University have estimated its maximum depth to be 113 m (371 ft) and its scale to be a third larger than Derinkuyu.

Therefore it seems that Derinkuyu is just part of a network of ancient subterranean lairs across Cappadocia. How far they reach and their buried histories remain part of an ongoing investigation.

# CHAPTER 2
# MYSTERIOUS MONUMENTS

Monoliths, mausoleums and pyramids, thousands of years old, stand as sentinels on the landscape, their purpose as opaque as their stone. Many experts have sought to unlock their secrets: excavating the soil, mapping their scale and measuring their alignment with the heavens. With no written records, we have had to glean their function by tracing the origin of stones, deciphering carvings and dating bone fragments. Was Türkiye's Göbekli Tepe the world's first temple? Were the pyramids aligned to match a constellation? Was England's Stonehenge an ancient observatory? While we have accumulated a degree of knowledge about these awe-inspiring edifices, they continue to tantalize, offering glimpses of ancient worlds. What do the human remains in the Plain of Jars in Laos reveal about millennia-old customs? What treasures are stored in the mausoleum of China's first emperor? What has historical research revealed about this grand necropolis and why are archaeologists afraid of entering it?

# WHY WAS STONEHENGE BUILT?

Stonehenge is perhaps the most famous megalithic construction in Europe. This ring of giant stones on Salisbury Plain in south-west England receives more than a million visitors every year. What special meaning did this place have for its builders? How were these huge stones hauled from hundreds of kilometres away, and for what purpose? There have been many theories over the centuries, some involving giants, Romans, Mycenaeans or Druids, and even the magician Merlin whisking the circle away from its earlier location in Ireland. Stonehenge's age, scale and mystery are all part of its draw.

The earliest written report of Stonehenge dates from around 1130CE. In his history of England, *Historia Anglorum*, Henry, Archdeacon of Huntingdon, described the site as follows: 'Stanenges, where the stones of wonderful size have been erected after the manner of doorways, so that doorway appears to have been raised upon doorway; and no one can conceive how such great stones have been so raised aloft, or why they were built there.' The name 'Stonehenge' comes from this period, from the Old English *stan* (stone) and *hencg* (hanging).

A more vivid account of the stones appeared a few years later. Around 1136, the medieval bishop and chronicler Geoffrey of Monmouth credited the legendary wizard Merlin with the construction in his book *Historia Regum Britanniae* (*The History of the Kings of Britain*). Supposedly, Merlin was instructed by King

Arthur's (page 209) uncle Aurelius Ambrosius to commemorate British nobles killed by Saxons, people from northern and central Germany, who invaded and settled in Britain during the 5th and 6th centuries. Merlin transported the circle intact from Ireland: 'If you want to grace the burial-place of these men with some lasting monument, send for the Giants' Ring which is on Mount Killaraus in Ireland. In that place there is a stone construction which no man of this period could ever erect...and there is no one alive strong

A 13th-century manuscript showing a giant positioning a lintel at Stonehenge.

enough to move them.' According to Geoffrey of Monmouth, the stones were originally imported from Africa by giants.

## EARLY EXCAVATION OF 'THE MOST NOTABLE ANTIQUITY'

The first excavations were undertaken in the 17th century, following a visit to the site in 1620 by King James I. Having first offered the owner, Robert Newdyk, a fair sum to purchase the site, the Duke of Buckingham was given permission to dig at its centre. Apparently, he only uncovered antlers, horns and charcoal. The king then instructed the architect Inigo Jones to draw up a plan of the site. Jones proceeded to describe Stonehenge in *The most notable Antiquity of Great Britain, vulgarly called Stonehenge on Salisbury Plain, restored by Inigo Jones Esquire* (1655) as of Roman design. He admired its symmetry and claimed it must have been dedicated to the Roman sky god Coelus. In his 1663 book *Chorea Gigantum*, Walter Charleton, King Charles II's physician, refuted the Roman origin and claimed that Stonehenge was built by the Danes, as 'a Court Royal or place for the Election and Inauguration of their Kings'. Charleton's supposition was based on descriptions of similar stone circles in Denmark.

The first scholar to give Stonehenge prehistoric provenance was the antiquarian John Aubrey, in 1665. Rather than attribute its construction to Romans, Saxons or Danes, Aubrey believed it was the work of the Druids, a Celtic priesthood described by Julius Caesar during his campaigns in western Europe (specifically his conquest of Gaul in 58–50BCE). He was supported in his conclusions 75 years later by the English doctor William Stukeley, who believed the site was a temple constructed around 460BCE by Phoenicians who founded the Druid religion. Stukeley was rather obsessed with Druids, fancying himself as an Arch-Druid named Chyndonax.

Despite interest in the site from modern-day Druids, their claim over Stonehenge is unsubstantiated. The priesthood is not thought to have existed at the time of Stonehenge's placement. While mistaken in his attribution of the monument, Stukeley provided many fine illustrations of the site and was the first to notice the stones' alignment with the Sun's movement during the solstices. If visitors were to stand in the middle of the stone circle on the year's longest day, they would see the Sun rise just to the left of the Heel Stone, an outlying stone just outside the circle. On the shortest day, the Sun would set between the two uprights of the tallest trilithon (two vertical stones with a vertical lintel stone).

On 3 January 1797 the report of one of the sarsen stones (sandstone boulders) and its lintel crashing to earth led to investigations by a local wool merchant and antiquary named William Cunnington. In his book *Ancient History of Wiltshire*, he included a more measured evaluation of studies of the site. His examination of what had been called a 'slaughter stone' proved it was not a flat table for sacrifices, but had originally stood upright.

## A NEOLITHIC SITE OF SIGNIFICANCE

Once the monument came into state ownership in 1918, a more thorough scientific excavation took place. As a result, Stonehenge as we know it was finally dated to around 2500BCE and a chronology of its development was worked out. What today's visitors see of Stonehenge is just part of the long history of the site. Long before the stones were raised, there were many 'long barrows' or communal graves surrounding the area, and earthworks of considerable size. One, known as the Greater Cursus, is a parallel pair of raised banks 3 km (2 miles) in length. This was clearly a location with great meaning for Britain's Neolithic people and one used for significant burials.

Excavations at Stonehenge itself have revealed constructions from around 2950BCE, when the site was a circular chalk bank and ditch 100 m (330 ft) in diameter, with a ring of small standing stones inside and an arrangement of 56 wooden posts. (Later, the post holes would be used to inter cremated human bones.) The ditch was dug with picks made from deer antlers, which were tossed aside when the work was completed. It would be another four centuries before something resembling today's stone circles were assembled.

## STONES OF VARYING COLOURS AND ORIGINS

The first of the stones we see today that were brought on site were not the large chiselled blocks that make up the outer ring of trilithons but the smaller 'bluestones' that form a more broken circle inside. These measure around 2 m (6.5 ft) in length and weigh an average 1.4 tonnes each. Made of dolerite, a dark rock that was once molten magma, these stones must have possessed some special importance for the builders of Stonehenge, because they had to be transported from south-west Wales. They may have considered the bluestones to have magical healing properties. Petrological studies have located their origin in the Preseli Hills, which are situated 220 km (137 miles) in a straight line from Stonehenge.

As for their transportation, experiments from the 1950s proved that it was possible for the stones to have been floated on rafts along rivers to within a handful of kilometres of Stonehenge. From the rivers they could have been dragged overland on sledges, using ropes woven from the inner bark of trees. Such an effort would have required a team working for 40 to 60 days. Markings on, and the shaping of, some of the stones suggest they may have been used as part of another monument before being brought to Stonehenge.

The bluestones were first arranged in two concentric circles on the site, before being moved to accommodate 30 large stones carved from sandstone boulders. These sarsen blocks, sourced much closer to home, measure up to 9 m (29.5 ft) in length and weigh about 36 tonnes. The stones are locked together using mortice and tenon joints – similar to the way carpenters would join timbers. A 3-km (2-mile) path of ditches and banks was then added. This so-called 'Stonehenge Avenue' joined the site to the River Avon.

Although the sarsens came from a quarry only around 25 km (16 miles) from Stonehenge, they were much larger and heavier than the bluestones and had to be moved over both hill and valley.

Stonehenge under the stars. Was it designed as a prehistoric observatory?

It probably required hundreds of people to lug each stone with ropes and wooden rollers. As for raising the stones into position, this could have been done by digging a hole and winching each stone with ropes over a timber A-frame. The lintels could have been placed on top by building a ramp to drag them upwards. The sarsens with their lintels would have formed an outer circle with 30 uprights, when completed. There is some doubt that the monument was finished as originally conceived, due to a shortage of large-enough stones.

These Neolithic builders showed great resource in removing and transporting the huge stones. And, according to research revealed in 2024, one stone on the site made a journey of about 750 km (466 miles). Studies of the 'altar stone' lying at the centre of the ring have identified it as coming from the north-east corner of Scotland. The old red sandstone block is part-buried at the heart of the monument, with two sarsens resting on top of it. It measures 5 m (16 ft) in length and weighs an estimated 6 tonnes. Experts examined the stone's chemical composition and the age of its minerals, and were able to match it with stones from an area between Inverness and the Orkney Islands in Scotland. How the stone was brought to southern England is unknown. A journey over sea or land would have been an incredible undertaking. One theory has it that the altar stone and the bluestones began their journeys towards Stonehenge far earlier, carried along by glaciers some 400,000 years ago.

## AN ANCIENT CEREMONIAL LANDSCAPE?

Stonehenge does not exist in isolation. It is part of a greater collection of Neolithic constructions – a vast 'ritual landscape'.

In walking distance from the site are round barrows containing fine grave goods. Around 3 km (2 miles) north of Stonehenge, Durrington Walls is an earthwork enclosure built around the time that the sarsen stones were placed at Stonehenge. Durrington Walls is almost 400 m (1,312 ft) across, with a 6 m (20 ft)-deep ditch and wooden uprights.

Not far south is Woodhenge, built of concentric circles of 24 timber posts. Was Woodhenge a model for Stonehenge? It has been suggested that both Durrington Walls and Woodhenge acted as ceremonial sites celebrating the living, while Stonehenge was built to celebrate ancestors. Animal bones found at Durrington Walls indicate that it was a setting for midwinter solstice feasting.

Another stone circle, known as Bluestonehenge, was erected 1.6 km (1 mile) away, along the banks of the River Avon. Close by was a small village that may have been used as accommodation for pilgrims, for the builders of the stone circles, or as a healing centre. Modern surveys using magnetometers (measuring changes in Earth's magnetic fields) and ground-penetrating radar have revealed the buried evidence of a further 15 stone circles, burial mounds and pits in the area.

While we now know much about the stones and how the monument was constructed, what about the people that raised it? What practices went on within the mysterious stone circle?

Many attempts have been made to identify the builders of Stonehenge. In 1953, the British archaeologist Richard Atkinson saw faint dagger shapes carved in one sarsen and was convinced they matched the work of the Mycenaeans from 2nd-century BCE Greece. Another 20th-century British archaeologist, Aubrey Burl, saw parallels with stone circles and tombs found in Brittany, France – particularly one rectangular carving. While there was contact between Neolithic Bretons and Britons, similar carvings found in Brittany predate the one in Stonehenge by a millennium.

The consensus is that Stonehenge was built by an ancient people of England, but for what purpose? Early assumptions were that it was purely a monument to the dead. Certainly, there are graves in and around the site: the bones of 63 men, women and children have been unearthed there. A Druidic temple was briefly proposed. Then, measurements of the site's alignments with the stars in the late 19th century led some scholars to suggest it would have been used as an astronomical calendar.

Early computer technology promoted further theories. Using an IBM 704 computer, the US astronomer Dr Gerald Hawkins generated evidence that the builders of Stonehenge could have used it to predict numerous solar and lunar events, such as eclipses. His theory, published in *Stonehenge Decoded* in 1966, has been dismissed as contrived or far-fetched. However, as William Stukeley realized, the axis of Stonehenge's central stones does align with the midsummer sunrise and midwinter sunset, as does that of Woodhenge. This provides a strong case for the henges to have been built for some ceremony during the solstices. This is certainly understood by the thousands of visitors who now turn up to the site to celebrate the longest day.

Excavations close to Stonehenge in the 1980s found the remains of ten cattle, several deer and a pig that had been butchered for major feasts, along with pots and tools. These remains were carbon-dated to between 3800 and 3700BCE, proving that Salisbury Plain was an important gathering place centuries before the building of Stonehenge. The site was commonly used for cremations, as evidenced by the ashes of 150 to 200 people cremated or placed there.

In 2002, a body was unearthed near this sacred centre, dating from about 2300BCE. The grave contained a figure in a foetal position surrounded by many treasures, including gold hair ornaments, copper knives, pottery, boar tusks and flint arrowheads. Variously called 'the Amesbury archer' or the 'king of Stonehenge', the figure, estimated to be between 35 and 45 years old, was thought to be a chieftain who originally came from northern Europe, possibly Switzerland. Injuries on his body suggest he may have travelled a great distance to benefit from Stonehenge's reputation as a healing centre. Therefore, Stonehenge may have been a memorial, a marker for the summer and winter solstices, a place of healing, or all three.

Stonehenge lost its importance as a gathering place some 3,500 years ago. Construction and modifications ceased, and it was left to the elements. Some stones toppled over. Several were re-erected in the 20th century and set in concrete bases. The meaning of the site was lost in memory. It requires the work of archaeologists to decode its form, by analyzing ripples in the landscape and buried bones in order to make sense of the monument. Stonehenge, for all its mystery, remains a magical place, luring pagans and partygoers to its circle. For thousands of years it has held a fascination for pilgrims hoping to make some connection with Britain's ancient past, and it will continue to do so.

# WHAT WAS THE PURPOSE OF THE PLAIN OF JARS?

About 400 km (248 miles) north-east of Vientiane, the capital of Laos, far away from the popular tourist route, is a 2,500-year-old mystery and what has been dubbed 'the world's most dangerous archaeological site'. Over hundreds of square kilometres in the rice paddies, forests and mountains around Phonsavan are scattered more than 2,000 bewildering stone urns. The area is known as the Plain of Jars, and we can only guess at the purpose of the receptacles found there from the somewhat grisly contents discovered inside them.

These tubular jars range in size from 60 cm (2 ft) tall and 85 cm (2.8 ft) wide to 3 m (10 ft) tall and 2 m (6.5 ft) wide, and weigh up to 31 tonnes. They seem to be randomly positioned, some on their own and others in clusters of several hundred. They date from prehistory, the Iron Age of Laos, between 1500BCE and 500BCE.

The jars are mostly carved from sandstone, with some made of limestone, granite or calcified coral. Analysis of the stone in the jars at one site (called 'Site 1') has identified its source as a quarry at Phukeng, some 8 km (5 miles) away. The discovery of several jars at various quarries suggests they were first carved among the stones. Then, they may have been dragged to the burial site using a pulley system, over wooden rollers, and pulled by elephant or buffalo.

While they vary in size, the jars are generally cylindrical in shape, widest at the bottom, with many featuring a rim for a lid. All but one are undecorated. The exception is a jar found to have a relief image of an amphibious human figure that has been described as a 'frog man'. A few jars retain stone lids. Several of these feature animal carvings, thought to be images of monkeys, tigers and frogs. It is possible that other jars had lids made from perishable materials, such as wood or rattan, that have not survived the centuries.

Locals have several theories about the use of the jars. One story is of an ancient king of giants named Khun Cheung, who celebrated victory over a great enemy with rice whiskey or *lau hai* brewed in the jars some 1,500 years ago. Another legend has a giant living in the mountains over Phonsavan, who would drain whiskey from the stone cups.

Site I in the Plain of Jars, Xieng Khuang province, north Laos.

## A TRANSFORMATIONAL TOOL FOR THE DEAD?

Human bones and ashes have been found in and around the jars, which suggests they had a role in funerary rites. The area may have been used as a burial site by travellers passing along an ancient trade route between the Mekong River and the Gulf of Tonkin in the South China Sea. It is also proposed that the jars collected rainwater for the caravans of traders.

There is evidence that the jars were used in an elaborate ritual in which a corpse was left to decay in one jar for some time, before being cremated and stored in a second jar. This idea is based on the traditional disposal of South-east Asian royals. In the past, royalty would have had their remains moved between a series of urns, following a belief that their soul was undergoing transformation on a path from the earthly domain to the spirit world. After several months, the body would then be cremated so their spirit could rise to heaven. Commoners, meanwhile, would be buried, their spirits remaining on Earth.

So far 127 sites of stone jars have been discovered, but only seven are open to tourists. Site 1 alone contains over 300 jars, with many more still being unearthed. Some of those found below ground are made of clay and full of soil, therefore too fragile to empty. Following many digs at the site which have revealed secondary burials of numerous persons, experts have estimated that the remains of 8,000 individuals may lie underground in and around Site 1.

Laos, like neighbouring Cambodia and Vietnam, suffered greatly during the Vietnam War between 1955 and 1975. Much land has still not been cleared of mines and unexploded ordnance. Beside the prescribed paths between the jars are red-and-white warning markers and roped-off areas. Phonsavan was below the flight path for US bombers and fighter jets during the war and an estimated 270 million cluster bombs were dumped in the region in a secret mission to destroy North Vietnamese supply routes. About 80 million bombs failed to detonate on impact and still claim hundreds of victims every year. It may take a century to clear Laos of these explosives. Evidence of their destruction is visible as craters on the ground and from shattered fragments or cracks in the ancient jars. The unexploded bombs remain a present danger to both local farmers and archaeologists keen to dig the site.

The Plain of Jars was studied in the early 1930s by Madeleine Colani, a French geologist and amateur archaeologist from the École Française d'Extrême-Orient. She investigated inside and around the jars and found human bone fragments, teeth, iron tools, coloured glass, spindle whorls (used for spinning), bronze jewellery, ceramic ear-discs, stone beads and charcoal. In a nearby limestone cave Colani discovered the walls were blackened from smoke. Two chimney holes had been cut into the cave ceiling to allow fumes to escape. She surmised that the cave was used as a crematorium and that ashes were then carried to the jars outside for storage.

Following Colani's work, excavations did not resume for several decades, largely due to the war and unexploded bombs at the site. In 1994, archaeologists returned and found burial pits beside the jars, some marked with limestone boulders. These contained bones, suggesting they were secondary burial sites, and that the deceased were first interred or placed in the stone urns to decompose before their bones were burned or placed elsewhere. Recent studies of the sediment beneath several stone jars has provided a range of dates for their positioning, from 1240 to 660BCE, with the jars and site being in continued use up to 500CE.

Laos is not unique in having such large stone mortuary containers. Similar jars have been discovered in Assam, in north-eastern India, and in Central Sulawesi, Indonesia, where large stone receptacles called *kalambas* contained the remains of whole families. There are also thought to be jar sites waiting to be found in Vietnam.

As work continues to clear the vast plot of deadly weapons, more land will become free for archaeological study. Currently less than 10 per cent of the 100 or so identified jar sites have been cleared for this purpose. Below ground there may be more urns, human remains and tools, which will provide a clearer picture of what the jars were used for. For now, it remains an enigma and mostly off-limits.

# WERE THE PYRAMIDS ALIGNED WITH THE STARS?

The only surviving wonder of the ancient world, the Great Pyramid of Giza is one of three pyramids forming a necropolis built for ancient Egyptian pharaohs of the Fourth Dynasty between 2600 and 2500BCE. The faces of the pyramids, outside modern-day Cairo, are aligned with the cardinal points of a compass (north, east, south and west), but there may be more to their position than meets the eye. Were they deliberately built to reflect a specific constellation?

This was the proposition put forward by the Egyptian engineer and author Robert Bauval in 1994. He had been pondering the arrangement of the three great pyramids at Giza: the Great Pyramid of Khufu (*c.*2580–2560BCE), the Pyramid of Khafre (*c.*2570BCE) and Pyramid of Menkaure (*c.*2510BCE). While stargazing, he identified a correlation between the pyramids' positions and the 'belt' of Orion: a line of three bright stars in the constellation named after the mythical Greek hunter. One of the three pyramids was smaller and slightly out of line, just like the third of the three stars in Orion's Belt. While these pyramids were built for different pharaohs, to Bauval they appeared to be part of a singular plan.

Bauval found two other Fourth Dynasty pyramids he believed could take the place of significant stars in the constellation if their positions were projected on to the ground. He suggested the Pyramid of Djedefra at Abu Ruwash worked as Orion's 'left foot', while the Pyramid of Nebka at Zawyat al Aryan reflected Orion's 'right shoulder'. To complete his model of Orion in the sands, Bauval reasoned that other pyramids fitting the plan had been demolished or buried, or were never built. He eventually published his theory in a bestselling book, *The Orion Mystery*, with Adrian Gilbert.

## A BRIEF HISTORY OF PYRAMID BUILDING

The first pyramid to be built in ancient Egypt was the Step Pyramid at Saqqara (*c.*2670–2650BCE), designed to house the mummy of King Netjerikhet. The original plan was for a *mastaba*, or large rectangular stone structure above a burial chamber. Probably through the influence of the king's vizier (chief minister) Imhotep, the tomb gained further levels – a series of six colossal steps in total – to form a ziggurat-like pyramid 62.5 m (205 ft) high. It launched the Pyramid Age.

Sneferu, the first pharaoh of the Fourth Dynasty (2613–2589BCE) directed the building of three pyramids. His first, the Meidum pyramid, was originally planned as a steep seven-stepped pyramid, but poor foundations and construction led to it collapsing, possibly before completion. Despite this setback, Sneferu demanded an even greater monument be built at Dahshur, further north along the Nile. This was a more geometric pyramid with sides rising at 60-degree angles. Once again, ambition gave way to the forces of nature and the pyramid began to sink into the sand and shale below. Extra blocks of stone were placed around the base to shore up the crumbling edifice. The pyramid's architects revised the design, reducing the angle of the top half to 54 degrees. While the pyramid was completed, it was a patch-up job that came to be known as the 'Bent Pyramid', and unsuitable for the remains of a king.

The third attempt, the Red Pyramid (c.2590BCE) was less steep but it was the largest at 105 m (344 ft) high, and planted on more solid ground about a kilometre north of the Bent Pyramid. Originally covered by limestone, it was the first to be aligned to cardinal points, which was clearly important to its builders. Without compasses, the ancient Egyptians did not recognize a north pole, but worked out the direction of north from the movement of the stars around Alpha Draconis. (Due to the way Earth spins on its axis, at that time this star would have appeared as the pole star, around which others appear to move.) They managed to line up the pyramid to within less than one-tenth of a degree from geographic north. This pyramid would be the template for the next and greatest series of pyramids at Giza in both design and alignment.

Sneferu's son Khufu initiated a pyramid on a scale never before seen. Giza was chosen as the site for its strong limestone foundations and proximity to available stone and the Nile for transport. The architect for Khufu's grand project was the high priest, Hemiunu. The building of pyramids required all of his organizational skills. Much of the construction was undertaken by Egyptians conscripted for a few months at a time and housed at Heit el-Ghurab, a purpose-built settlement nearby, with its own butchers, bakeries and breweries. The workers respected their divine king, whose role it was to commune with the gods and ensure the prosperity of the country. They laboured in competing teams and were well fed, although injuries were likely due to the backbreaking nature of the work. It has been calculated that teams in the thousands working for ten-hour days would have needed to place a 1-tonne block of stone every two minutes, in order to erect the Great Pyramid within 20 years. There are thought to be about 2.3 million such blocks in the Great Pyramid of Khufu alone.

At 147 m (481 ft), when originally clad in limestone, the Great Pyramid of Khufu was for 3,800 years the tallest building in the world. There are at least three chambers inside: one unfinished subterranean chamber and two others raised from the ground. From the pyramid entrance, a corridor leads downwards then splits, with one route moving through a tall Grand Gallery. This corridor also divides, with one route leading to the misnamed Queen's Chamber and the other to the King's Chamber. These are spartan and were emptied by tomb robbers in antiquity. In the King's Chamber is a large, unmarked and empty granite sarcophagus and the beginnings of two shafts directed to the north and south of the chamber.

These tight and straight channels, about 20 cm by 20 cm (8 in by 8 in) in cross-section, were first thought to be ventilation shafts, although their ends are blocked off. In 1964 Alexander Badway, an Egyptian scholar of ancient Egyptian art and architecture at the University of California, suggested they were designed as pathways to guide the pharaoh's *ka* or spirit towards the stars. Victoria Trimble, astronomer and professor of physics at the University of California, calculated that during the period the Great Pyramid was built, the northern shaft would align with Alpha Draconis and the southern shaft would capture Orion's Belt as it passed across the sky. A shaft from the Queen's Chamber was thought to point to the bright star Sirius in Canis Major, understood by the ancient Egyptians to represent Isis, the consort of Osiris.

Following Khufu's death, his first son Djedefre built his own pyramid at Abu Rawash, 8 km (5 miles) north of Giza (the supposed 'left foot' of Orion). Little remains of this, due to it being plundered for building materials. Djedefre's brother Khafre was

The Giza necropolis, Cairo, Egypt.

next to the throne. The Pyramid of Khafre at Giza (supposedly reflecting Orion's Belt) is smaller than his father's, although it appears larger due to its elevated foundation and retains some of its original limestone cover. Khafre is also credited for the construction of the Great Sphinx. The pyramid built for Khafre's son, Menkaure (also supposedly reflecting a belt star) is less than half the height of the Great Pyramid of Khufu. All three Pyramids of Giza, like the Red Pyramid at Dahshur, are accurately aligned with the cardinal points.

## THE SIGNIFICANCE OF ORION TO ANCIENT EGYPT

Clearly, the comparison between the Pyramids of Giza and Orion's Belt was not a random choice for Robert Bauval. The ancient Egyptians were able astronomers before the invention of telescopes and there are many images and hieroglyphs on the walls inside pyramids from later dynasties depicting rituals involving the stars. These 'Pyramid Texts' describe pharaohs ascending to the heavens on their death and even becoming stars. Ancient Egyptians believed Osiris, their god of the dead, resided in Orion. The texts also claim 'these pyramids of theirs are Orion-Osiris', a direct correlation between the monuments and the god in the stars. Bauval and Gilbert's notion that the Giza necropolis was linked to constellations was supported by the ancient names of the pyramids. The Pyramid of Nebka was once called 'Nebka is a Star', while the Pyramid of Djedefra was identified as 'Djedefra is a Sehedu Star'. The Great Pyramid of Khufu was called 'The Horizon of Khufu'.

While most archaeologists and academic Egyptologists were hesitant about backing Bauval and Gilbert's claims, Iorweth Edwards, a noted Egyptologist and curator in the British Museum's

Department of Egyptian Antiquities, agreed that one shaft may have been deliberately aligned with Orion, as did Jaromir Malek, Director of the Griffith Institute for Egyptology at Oxford University.

The link between the pharaohs and Orion was compelling, but the idea that the pyramids were meant to mirror the position of the stars was less credible. Bauval and Gilbert claimed that the Pyramids of Giza were set 38 degrees from the north, perfectly matching Orion's Belt in 10500BCE, a scarcely credible date when they claim the layout of Giza was planned; however, astronomers proved that the belt was actually angled at 50 degrees. The authors could not convincingly match any other of the numerous pyramids across Egypt with a constellation. Neither was a later attempt to associate the Great Sphinx with the constellation of Leo plausible, since the zodiac was not recognized in Egypt at the time the Sphinx was built.

Even Bauval and Gilbert's ground map of Orion was not to scale, apart from the belt itself, which they had inverted to match the heavens. Robert Chadwick, an ancient Near Eastern historian from Bishop's University, Canada, commented, 'Robert Bauval and Adrian Gilbert never succeed in matching more than three pyramids to three stars at any one time. Since there are thirty pyramids in the region between Abu Rawash and Dahshur, this supposed match-up is serendipitous and may be attributed to chance rather than some kind of master plan devised by the ancient Egyptians of the Fourth Dynasty.'

In the late 1990s, astronomers Anthony Fairall, from the University of Cape Town, and Ed Krupp, from Griffith Observatory in Los Angeles, checked Bauval and Gilbert's calculations and the positioning of Orion's Belt in the 3rd millennium BCE. Unlike Victoria Trimble's earlier assessments, their conclusions were not supportive.

Orion's Belt consists of three bright stars, Alnitak, Alnilam and Mintaka.

On the layout of the Pyramids of Giza, Krupp wrote: 'For all I know, they may symbolize the Three Blind Mice, the Three Graces, the Three Musketeers, the Three Wise Men, or the Three Stooges. But I don't think they are the three stars of Orion's Belt.'

Bauval and Gilbert's attempt to map what we understand as the constellation of Orion drew a lot of interest and led to more unorthodox theories. The correlation between the three large pyramids at Giza and the stars in Orion's Belt, and theories on the use of the shafts for directing the spirit of the pharaoh from

Khufu's pyramid, are still persuasive ideas. The ancient Egyptians certainly attributed great importance to these stars. While they may not have duplicated all of the constellation of Orion as we understand it, they may have sought to complement the three stars of the belt through the position of their most important edifices – royal burial tombs. While wider opinions regarding a complete network of constellations spread either side of the Nile have been dismissed as a fringe theory, this element of Bauval and Gilbert's thesis is still worth contemplating.

The desert sands are deep. New tombs and hieroglyphs may yet be discovered that provide a clear guide to the architecture of the pharaohs. Even 4,500 years after they were built, the Great Pyramids can still yield surprises and new ways of interpreting their design. Whether or not they reflect constellations, they are true wonders of the world.

# WHAT AWAITS IN THE TOMB OF CHINA'S FIRST EMPEROR?

It was one of the most astonishing archaeological discoveries of the 20th century. Hidden underground, thousands of clay soldiers lined up in ranks to protect China's first emperor throughout his rule in the afterlife, in a phenomenal display of power and desire for immortality. What's more, the vast trenches of underworld guards are only a teaser for another magnificent monument – the tomb of the first emperor himself. Who was the man who unified China and became its all-powerful ruler? Why did he order the construction of 8,000 terracotta troops? And why does his huge tomb remain undisturbed?

For centuries, a low mound east of the modern city of Xi'an in north-central China had been ignored by local farmers. Just 43 m (141 ft) high and studded with trees, Mount Li was just another feature of the landscape. Occasionally, fragments of pottery were unearthed there, but little was thought of them. Then, in March 1974, six peasant-farmer brothers named Wang, while digging for a well during a drought, hit upon a collection of broken, life-size figures, some still partly painted and bearing bronze weapons. The bronze was valuable and collected to sell for recycling. Fortunately, the farmers' boss discovered the cache and realized it was of greater archaeological worth. Little did any of them know that the most astounding trove from antiquity would spring from this well: a 2,200-year-old terracotta army.

## THE RISE OF THE FIRST EMPEROR

From the 5th to the 3rd century BCE, China was a land of small, warring states where rival lords vied for supremacy. In 316BCE, King Hui of Qin (in north-western China) won a decisive victory by taking control of Sichuan, thereby doubling his territory and gaining new lands rich in minerals and cereals. Hui was quick to assert control over his new kingdom. He instituted a division of counties and administrative areas, within which registration of families was compulsory, laws were strictly enforced, and weight, measures, coins and the calendar were standardized. This organization and efficiency extended to Hui's armies. While they were no better armed than their foes, they comprised mostly professional soldiers who were disciplined, well fed and highly mobile.

Hui's successor Zhaoxiang continued the expansion of the kingdom, conquering the Chu (the Qin's main rival for dominance) around 278BCE. In 247BCE, 13-year-old Zheng ascended the throne, which he took over officially when he came of age in 238BCE. Zheng inherited a mighty empire and expanded it further, marching on to claim the states of the Han, Zhao, Wei, Chu, Yan and Qi in quick succession. The country was finally unified in 221BCE and would be known in the west as China, from this first dynasty, Qin. With all former warring states under his control, Zheng felt due a title that befitted his position as sole ruler. He chose Qin Shi Huang, meaning 'first august emperor of the Qin, the first emperor of China'.

## A STAGGERINGLY LARGE WORKFORCE

The tight bureaucracy of the Qin state was extended across its new territories. The population was heavily monitored and threatened with severe punishment for any disobedience. The conquered armies were disbanded and their weapons melted down for use in 12 giant statues commemorating the new emperor. Emperor Qin Shi Huang was now able to mobilize one of history's largest workforces. Criminals made up the majority of the labour force along with hundreds of thousands of soldiers, no longer needed in battle. Every male between the ages of 15 and 60 was declared eligible. In total, a million or more people may have been directed towards building the emperor's pet projects.

This workforce laid a network of roads spanning the new nation: an estimated 6,750 km (4,200 miles) of earthen thoroughfares, including an 800-km (500-mile) road between the (then) capital Xianyang and northern military bases. Other construction works included the building of five palaces, nine command depots, and the refortification of an earthwork Great Wall to hold back the 'barbarians' in the north. (The wall was as much repair as new construction and would be reinforced and extended by later dynasties.) Of the palaces, Epang (just west of Xi'an), was to be the most magnificent: its throne room measured 690 m (2,300 ft) by 115 m (377 ft), providing enough space to seat 10,000 people. It was to be joined by a covered walkway of 10 km (6 miles) in length to an administrative building. This monumental palace was uncompleted in Qin Shi Huang's lifetime, and was destroyed by fire during the rebellion that ended the Qin dynasty in 206 BCE.

It is said that the first emperor took control of history by demanding the burning of books in 213 BCE, to remove the influence of old philosophies. However, bamboo books on medicine, divination and agriculture survived these conflagrations, and the effect of the ban was less than legend suggests. The story of book burning may indeed have been a deliberate exaggeration provided by historians under a later dynasty a century later.

Perhaps the greatest of Qin Shi Huang's projects was one not meant to be appreciated by human eyes. Even before his succession, the young ruler was considering his legacy. In 246 BCE, just a year after his ascendancy, he ordered the excavation of a mountain for his own magnificent tomb. The site chosen was Mount Li, 40 km (25 miles) east of Xi'an, close to where his ancestors were buried.

It was believed at the time that people had two souls: a creative spirit that escaped to the realm of immortals upon death and an earthen soul that remained buried. It was also understood that the dead could continue to make use of items buried with them, even if they were only figurative. It's for this reason that the most powerful rulers were interred with grave goods, including weapons, pottery, jewellery and even servants. The ruler's retinue were sometimes killed or buried alive with their lord. For the first Emperor of China, nothing less than an army would be sufficient to accompany him into the afterlife.

## EQUIPPING AN ARMY FOR THE AFTERLIFE

The Terracotta Army, as it would become known, consists of an estimated 8,000 full-size figures shaped in clay – an army meant to last an eternity. There are infantry soldiers carrying swords, lances and spears, kneeling archers, 130 chariots with 520 clay horses, 150 cavalry horses with attendant grooms, plus musicians, acrobats and even one bulky wrestler. The figures are arranged in several deep pits, the largest of which is 60 m (197 ft) long, 62 m (203 ft) wide and about 9 m (29 ft) deep.

Mass-production methods were used to assemble such a prodigious number of figures; craftspeople created identical clay figures that were hardened in kilns, pieced together, dressed in various armours cast in clay and provided with real weapons. The soldiers have an average height of 1.77 m (5 ft 10 in), with officers and generals given extra height that they may not have possessed in real life. Each figure weighs up to 272 kg (600 lb).

Every one of the terracotta soldiers has a slightly different face: all are handsome and unblemished but decorated with subtle turns

Terracotta warriors inside the Qin Shi Huang Mausoleum.

of eyebrow, moustache and beard. Hair is styled in a range of topknots that denote status. The soldiers share the same impassive expression, while uniforms vary to show rank, with a range of caps, collars, buckles and tassels. The moulded armour reflects the period's strapped leather plates over vests and wraparound coats. Many statues bear the stamps or signatures of their makers. The figures were originally brightly painted and lacquered, but little of the original colour has survived.

Other workers shaped and cast the army's weapons in bronze. Many animals and other models were sculpted too, including 46 fine birds such as cranes, swans and geese. Skeletons of 31 real birds were also found in clay coffins. There were also human remains entombed nearby, including many bodies with limbs cut off and over 100 executed convict labourers.

Following the initial finds, orderly excavations began on the first of the Terracotta Army pits in 1974. Layers of soil and gravel had to be removed before the lengthy task of recording the shards of clay and rebuilding the figures – an extremely complex jigsaw puzzle. Not one clay figure was found intact and each one took about a year to reconstruct. A smaller pit was discovered during a second phase of work between 1975 and 1976, and a third in 1977. A fourth pit was also uncovered, but this was empty, presumably because the emperor's early death did not allow enough time for work to be completed.

The mausoleum containing the Terracotta Army opened as a museum on 1 October 1979, with visitors able to view Pit 1. Its planners completely underestimated the interest in the site and there were not enough facilities to cope with the tens of thousands who arrived every day to see this incredible mausoleum for themselves. More funds were forthcoming, further pits opened for viewing, and the museum expanded accordingly.

In 2011, archaeologists found nine tombs in a deep pit at the vast mausoleum site. The coffins were removed from the site for safekeeping in 2024. Among them was a coffin weighing 16 tonnes above a funerary collection of weapons, armour, jade, gold and silver camel figurines, and over 6,000 bronze coins. Experts believe this may be either the final resting place of Prince Gao, one of Emperor Qin Shi Huang's 50 children, or that of a general or high-ranking official. Gao is recorded as having regretted not voluntarily following his father into the afterlife after the emperor's death; Qin Shi Huang's heir and youngest son, Hu Hai, was happy to arrange his brother's killing and burial in the mausoleum.

# A PALATIAL UNDERGROUND TOMB

The Terracotta Army stand guard east of the first emperor's mausoleum. While the clay warriors have become a major draw for visitors, what of the tomb itself? We have descriptions of its construction written by the Han historian Sima Qian a century later. Curiously, though, he makes no mention of the clay army assembled in a neighbouring pit in his record, noting:

'Digging and preparation work at Mount Li began when the First Emperor first came to the throne. Later, after he had unified his empire, 700,000 men were sent there from all over his empire. They dug through three layers of groundwater, and poured in bronze for the outer coffin. Palaces and scenic towers for a hundred officials were constructed, and the tomb was filled with rare artefacts and wonderful treasure. Craftsmen were ordered to make crossbows and arrows primed to shoot at anyone who enters the tomb. Mercury was used to simulate the hundred rivers, the Yangtze, Yellow River and the great sea, and set to flow mechanically. Above were representation of the heavenly constellations, below, the features of the land. Candles were made from fat of "man-fish", which is calculated to burn and not extinguish for a long time.'

As described, workers initially dug down to freshwater springs and built drains to prevent the tomb flooding. The ceiling was decorated with pearls to reflect the night sky. Lamps were fuelled with what is believed to be whale oil. Non-invasive studies of the tomb have measured the underground palace at 460 m (1,500 ft) by 390 m (1,300 ft). It is surrounded by a brick wall and above this is a 40-m (130-ft) high earthen wall with passageways leading to the perimeter. The tomb chamber is 80 m (260 ft) by 50 m (160 ft) and about 15 m (50 ft) high. Matching Sima Qian's reports, scans have confirmed high levels of mercury within the tomb, although this may be due to the use of ground cinnabar (a sulphide of mercury) used as a red pigment for decoration. Above ground, space was allocated for Qin Shi Huang's descendants to perform rituals in his honour.

Qin Shi Huang's heir ordered that all of the emperor's concubines who had not borne him children should be killed and buried with him. To ensure the secrets of the tomb remained so, all of those who had worked on the mausoleum were also sealed inside, possibly while still alive.

The tomb would be occupied much sooner than the first emperor had anticipated. In 211BCE, a meteorite landed in the lower reaches of the Yellow River. It was found with the message, 'The First Emperor will die and his land will be divided' etched on to it. The emperor demanded an investigation but no one dared admit they had added the message, so everyone in the local village was executed and the rock was destroyed.

In the last years of his life the emperor became paranoid about assassination (records show at least three attempts were made on his life) and kept his movements secret. Years earlier, he had ordered many of his scholars to be put to death after reports of his comings and goings were shared between them. As well as fearing death, Qin Shi Huang was obsessed with achieving immortality. He was prescribed elixirs by various physicians to extend his life. Ironically, it may have been the toxic cinnabar in one of these that slowly poisoned him.

During the fourth of his lengthy inspection tours of the nation, on 10 September 210BCE, Emperor Qin Shi Huang died aged 49, just 11 years into his imperial reign. Rotting fish were transported alongside the first emperor's body, to mask the smell of his decomposing corpse on its 450-km (280-mile), month-long journey back to the capital, Xianyang.

It would take 38 years to complete the emperor's tomb. In 209BCE, rebellions erupted in the defeated territories and tomb workers had to be diverted to army duties. The trouble reached the tomb complex where overground buildings were ransacked and a fire started in one of the terracotta warrior pits. This may have helped cause the collapse of roofing timbers, which crushed the clay soldiers. The Qin Dynasty would last just two more years, ending with the surrender and execution of Ying Ziying in 206BCE.

Excavations of the tomb have been put on hold for 50 years to limit potential damage to the priceless historical treasure. When exposed to the air, moisture caused the terracotta figures to be affected by mould and procedures to dry the chambers where they were stored led to remaining lacquer coatings peeling off, along with any paint. There are fears that a similar fate could ruin artefacts stored in the first emperor's tomb: paper, silk and textiles are especially vulnerable

A stepped path over the mound of the Mausoleum of the First Qin Emperor.

materials. As for physical harm to the archaeologists who would carry out excavations, it's thought that the rumoured rivers of mercury, while toxic, do not present too much of a risk. And, if they exist, the crossbow booby traps designed to kill tomb raiders were made of wood, so are likely to have rotted away. Scientists continue to develop methods that could preserve any finds for posterity and an eventual investigation of the tomb is likely to happen but, with such an historic prize on offer, caution prevails.

The Terracotta Army (as The Emperor Qin Shi Huang's Mausoleum Site Museum is widely known) is now the second-most-visited tourist site in China. What is seen by visitors, while overwhelming, is just a small part of the afterlife realm ordered by Qin Shi Huang, First Emperor of China. His own tomb remains unsullied. A stone pathway allows visitors to ascend to its height but the certain riches within are untouched. It is a wonder waiting to be revealed and perhaps the real mystery is how long we must wait until scientific advancement allows us to look inside.

# IS GÖBEKLI TEPE THE WORLD'S FIRST TEMPLE?

The 'Fertile Crescent', a sweep of land spanning a number of countries in the Middle East and fed by the Euphrates, Tigris and Nile rivers, is considered one of the cradles of civilization: where agriculture began, plants and animals were domesticated, and the first towns were built. On its northern edge, in the Taurus mountains of south-eastern Türkiye, archaeologists uncovered Göbekli Tepe, a Neolithic site that defied explanation. Within this complex they discovered buried circular rooms dominated by T-shaped stone blocks carved with reliefs of predatory animals, plus modified human bone fragments among the debris. Was Göbekli Tepe the site of some unknown animal or skull cult?

Göbekli Tepe ('Belly Hill' in Turkish) is located on a rise situated around 10 km (6 miles) north-east of the city of Urfa. The mound excavated by archaeologists provided a commanding view over the Mesopotamian plains, but it was not entirely natural. It was around 300 m (1,000 ft) in diameter, and raised by about 15 m (48 ft) due to debris left by humans, including rubble, charcoal, ashes and animal bones. The site was examined in detail by the German archaeologist Klaus Schmidt for 20 years from 1995. Beneath the mound, his team uncovered five rooms: four circular in nature, the largest of which is 30 m (100 ft) across. The fifth and most recently built room is rectangular.

The chambers were filled with detritus including stone tools and bones, probably as a result of a slope collapsing. This debris filling was used to date the sites to between 9500BCE and 8000BCE. The earliest date places the construction of Göbekli Tepe shortly after the end of the last Ice Age and about 6,000 years before Stonehenge (page 79) was built. This Neolithic period also predates the advent of pottery and metalwork in the region.

Once the debris was removed, two tall, T-shaped limestone megaliths were revealed in the centre of each circular enclosure. These pillars are up to 5m (16 ft) in height and weigh between 7 and 10 tonnes. Further, smaller standing stones pointed inwards from the drystone wall encircling each room. The floors were paved with limestone mortar or plaster. Some rooms included stone benches.

Three similar T-shaped pillars were found at a quarry site, indicating that the pillars were cut from a hilltop about 100 m (330 ft) from the excavation site. Flint and bone tools would have to have been used for such a huge task. The largest cut stone was 7 m (23 ft) long and estimated to weigh about 50 tonnes. There are thought to be at least another 16 Neolithic rings within the 9 hectares (22 acres) of Göbekli Tepe, each featuring eight pillars.

The Göbekli Tepe pillars are considered the oldest megaliths in the world. Quarrying, moving and placing the stones would have required the collaboration of a large workforce at a time when people were hunter-gatherers. Some experts estimate it would have taken 50 to 75 people to move each stone. They must have agreed a purpose for the building, based on sharing a need or spiritual belief. This upsets standard theories that human societies have to

A circular chamber uncovered at Göbekli Tepe, Türkiye.

settle first and begin farming to provide a surplus, before spending time on more abstract pursuits. Göbekli Tepe seems to show that even hunter-gatherers could devote themselves to communal constructions and religious purposes.

The obvious question is what was the site's purpose? In 2017, pieces of human skulls were located on the site. These fragments included deliberate cuts and holes, as if they had been tampered with after death. The flesh had been removed, modifications made and, possibly, pigments added. These decorated human skulls may have been put on display in the chambers. Some experts see this as a sign that Göbekli Tepe was a base for a 'skull cult' that showed off the decapitated heads of its enemies or venerated those of respected ancestors.

## FIRST-EVER TEMPLE?

As the glaciers receded from the Fertile Crescent at the end of the last Ice Age, some 11,000 years ago, rainfall increased and plants began to thrive on once-frozen land. With food now plentiful, the first human settlements began to appear here as people turned from a nomadic hunter-gatherer lifestyle to one involving the cultivation of crops and animal domestication. This 'agricultural revolution' was in fact a gradual process that took place over 8,000 years.

When Göbekli Tepe was constructed, the global human population was estimated to be five to six million. It would be another 6,000 years before writing appeared, so researchers had to look for clues to the purpose of the complex by interpreting images carved on the pillars and statues. Most of these depict male predatory animals, including lions, bulls, gazelles, wild sheep, boars and foxes, as well as snakes, spiders, scorpions and vultures. Few of these were the type of animals hunted by humans for food. Were these reliefs meant to depict animal spirits and ward off danger?

Some of these images appear to have been carved over earlier reliefs that were scratched away. In addition, some of the T-shaped pillars feature human arms carved into the bottom halves, with a few figures dressed in loincloths. This suggests that they represent human figures – possibly ancestors. If this was a religious site, it could comfortably claim the title given to it by Klaus Schmidt as the 'world's first temple'. Schmidt also believed that the chambers he found were deliberately filled in and covered up, although this idea has since been dismissed.

Since Schmidt's death in 2014, deeper excavations have found signs of settlement around the site, including domestic tools and drains for channelling rainwater to cisterns. In the Neolithic

Predatory animal reliefs on stones uncovered at Göbekli Tepe.

period, 11,000 years ago, the surrounding hills would have provided plentiful wild cereals, such as einkorn wheat and barley. As evidenced by the discovery of 7,000 grinding stones, these cereals would have been used for porridge and beer or as fodder for livestock, although it's not clear whether or not they were also cultivated. Charcoal found at the site has been identified as belonging to pistachio and almond trees.

Animal-bone fragments found at Göbekli Tepe show that animals were butchered and cooked. More than 60 per cent of the bones were from the gazelles that would have passed through the area seasonally; there were also bones from boar, sheep, red deer, vultures, cranes, ducks and geese. The preponderance of bones from wild animals and birds suggests that the people of Göbekli Tepe had not yet moved on to domesticating animals.

## HUNTING, GATHERING AND WORSHIPPING?

Having the capacity to direct labour towards less functional building indicates that the people that lived in Göbekli Tepe did not lack for food. They had enough free time away from foraging, and possibly farming to perform or attend ceremonies. Alternatively, they may have considered their beliefs to be of paramount importance. It's also likely that the site was used by more than one local settlement. Nor are the T-shaped stones unique to Göbekli Tepe: similar structures have been found at Nevalı Çori, a site about 60 km (36 miles) north-west. The same iconography was used at other locations, including the nearby archaeological site of Karahan Tepe. Clearly, whatever the purpose of Göbekli Tepe, it formed part of a widespread culture. However, at some point during the 8th millennium BCE, the enclosures fell out of use. Bones and gravel from the slopes around the enclosures tumbled in and hid the monuments from sight.

Göbekli Tepe and its surrounds are hugely interesting for archaeologists, but so far only about 5 per cent of the sites here have been excavated. There is hope that, with further investigation, in the years to come we may understand the very early prehistoric culture that fashioned these puzzling chambers.

# WHAT HIDES BENEATH THE TEMPLE OF THE FEATHERED SERPENT?

Around 50 km (30 miles) north-east of Mexico City lie the remains of one of pre-Columbian Mexico's greatest civilizations, and the largest American city of its time. Settled around 400BCE, Teotihuacán was already abandoned by the time the Aztecs found it. The Aztecs named it Teotihuacán (pronounced 'tay-oh-tee-wah-KAHN'), meaning 'the place where the gods were born'. The city, with its richly carved pyramids and plazas, linked by the Avenue of the Dead, hid many secrets but it was only properly excavated in the early 20th century. Archaeologists swept away centuries of dust and rubble, revealing fine murals and indecipherable hieroglyphs, before one of the city's greatest secrets was discovered by chance. In 2003 a heavy rainstorm caused a courtyard in the centre of the city to collapse, opening a passageway that appeared to go underneath the ancient Temple of the Feathered Serpent. Would this exciting discovery finally unravel the enigma of this 2,000-year-old pyramid, and the people that built it?

Some time around the 4th century BCE, the Mexican basin was occupied by small farming communities, possibly the Totonacs, a tribe from the east. These communities gathered around the springs of what is now Teotihuacán and began working obsidian, a green-tinted, black volcanic glass, into cutting tools. This obsidian must have seemed to have been delivered by the gods; it would provide spearheads for a large army and become a lucrative export.

## A MONUMENTAL URBAN CENTRE

By 1BCE, an estimated population of 40,000 to 50,000 had turned the site into a sizeable city with 23 temple complexes and a centre built around a road named the Miccaotli, running for 2.4 km (1.5 miles) with a roughly north–south axis pointed towards the sacred volcano Cerro Gordo. This road was later named the Avenue of the Dead (Calle de los Muertos), although it contains no notable tombs. Beside this thoroughfare stood two magnificent pyramids, today known as the Pyramids of the Sun and the Moon. The Pyramid of the Sun is the third-largest pyramid in the world: at 219 m by 232 m (719 ft by 761 ft), its base is as large as Egypt's Great Pyramid of Khufu, and it reaches a height of 65 m (213 ft).

Teotihuacán expanded its power over the next few centuries, as more territory was claimed to support a growing population. To the south, in Las Pilas, there is evidence of large-scale cotton production. By 250CE, Teotihuacán's reach included the Zapotec capital of Monte Albán in the Oaxaca Valley. There, its people could trade for mica, a glassy mineral that was precious enough to the Teotihuacános that they buried sheets of it below their pyramids.

Along with trading and political expansion, the city of Teotihuacán expanded over the next 650 years, with the notable construction of the Temple of the Feathered Serpent, a pyramid dedicated to the creator god Quetzalcoatl. This was positioned at the southern end of the city's main road. Only the ornate western façade remains today from the original building. Beside the steps that rise to its peak are numerous serpent heads and reliefs, featuring the goggle-eyes of the rain god Tlaloc. They are placed in a watery setting and decorated with shells. Some of the original paint is still visible.

The sunken plaza outside the temple, known as the Citadel (Ciudadela), was designed so that it could be flooded as a re-creation of the sea from which the world and all life sprang, according to creation myths of the period. The temple itself may have been a

The Temple of the Feathered Serpent, Teotihuacán, Mexico.

representation of the Sacred Mountain which rose from the waters at the beginning of time, according to Mesoamerican origin myths. Stone-walled canals were constructed to steer the course of the San Juan River away from monuments including this temple.

Many of the city's buildings were decorated with red fresco murals of gods and animals. Apartment compounds were built around the religious and administrative centre. These blocks could accommodate over 2,000 people, with 60 to 100 individuals living in a series of connected rooms based around a courtyard. The quarters contained kitchens, shrines and storerooms. There is a great variety in size and comfort within these apartments, with some fine enough to be described as palaces while others are more like cramped rooms.

Teotihuacán thrived by trading obsidian tools and fine, polished 'Thin Orange' ceramics across what is now Mexico. It had contact with the contemporary Maya capitals Tikal (modern Guatemala) and Copán (modern Honduras). Outside the city, people grew crops on raised fields in lakes and swamps and in fertile volcanic soil, including beans, avocados, peppers and squash, while also raising chickens and turkeys.

At its peak around 650CE, Teotihuacán covered an area of 21 sq km (8 square miles), greater than the imperial city of Rome. It was the largest city in the Americas at the time, and may have accommodated 150,000 people. And then, within a century, the city saw waves of destruction, with major buildings and artworks set aflame and wrecked, and the population scattered to villages away from the urban centre. This may have been the result of an uprising against the ruling elite, or an invasion from outside the city. Teotihuacán may also have suffered from long-lasting droughts and famines triggered by the eruption of the Ilopango volcano in today's El Salvador, around 431CE. Eventually, only a few thousand squatters remained. It was this shadow of a city that the Aztecs encountered when they moved into the area in the 1300s.

## MYSTERIOUS COMMUNICATIONS

Who were the people of Teotihuacán and what did they believe? The builders of this vast city had a written language based on hieroglyphs, although this is yet to be deciphered and it may only have recorded names and dates. The monuments that they left show the Teotihuacános had many gods, with the greatest of them all being a female deity described as a spider. They also worshipped Tlaloc (the rain god), Xipe Totec (the god of spring), and Quetzalcoatl, a god that represented fertility and was often depicted as a giant feathered snake.

Sacrifices of both animals and people were offered to these gods. The evidence for this was found in 1989, when archaeologists unearthed the remains of 18 victims in a pit south of the Temple of the Feathered Serpent (Quetzalcoatl). Another 200 human sacrifices were made when the temple was built in the 3rd century CE, most of whom were soldiers, perhaps from a defeated army. The bodies of more victims were found in a burial vault in the Pyramid of the Moon, some bound and decapitated. Animal sacrifices included canines, jungle cats and eagles.

It was presumed that the Temple of the Feathered Serpent was built on solid rock and there was nothing to investigate beneath it. Then, the storm of 2003 caused a sinkhole to appear in its courtyard. A Mexican archaeologist, Sergio Gómez Chávez, was the first to look inside. He discovered a human-built tunnel blocked at both ends by large rocks. The area was scanned by high-resolution, ground-penetrating radar to produce a map of the underground lair.

A similar tunnel discovered below the Temple of the Sun had been looted before archaeologists reached it, whereas this new passage below the Feathered Serpent pyramid promised to be unspoiled. Permission was granted for a dig in 2009. The work excavating it was painstaking, with nearly 1,000 tonnes of earth needing to be removed. Early finds in the tunnel included large conch shells decorated with deities, fine necklaces, figurines, pottery and even pieces of human skin. These appear to have been left deliberately as sacrificial offerings.

About 15 m (50 ft) inside the tunnel, the metal called pyrite or 'fool's gold' was detected in the walls. This glistened under torchlight, producing the effect of standing beneath the stars. Beyond this, some 17 m (55 ft) below ground, was a mound that represented a mountain with pools of mercury as lakes, both features matching the design of the temple and its plaza above ground. Here too was a depiction of the creation and arrangement of the cosmos. The subterranean space is thought to have been planned as a virtual underworld.

The tunnel led to a cross-shaped chamber and it was here that the finest treasures were located, including a quartet of greenstone figures of shamans. There were also sculptures of jaguars, inlaid wooden masks, greenstone crocodile teeth, balls of amber, and boxes filled with iridescent beetle wings.

The Temple of the Feathered Serpent may be understood as an illustration of the centre of the world, rising like a mountain from the waters at the dawn of time. And, for centuries, the Teotihuacános were the centre of their own world, as the dominant power in Mesoamerica. They built the greatest city in the western hemisphere 1,300 years ago, which then fell apart. Much is still to be understood about a civilization that left no clear written record except its incredible monuments, which still have a scale and power that draws in millions curious about those who paved the Avenue of the Dead.

# CHAPTER 3
# ARCANE ARTEFACTS

Every so often archaeology exhumes something that confounds all expectations: an object of such fine craft that it seems beyond the capability of the era it came from. Relics with major spiritual or occult significance are brought to light, dividing opinion and being either venerated as icons or denounced as fakes. Can the millennia-old directions on a copper scroll found in a cave lead archaeologists to long-lost temple treasures in the deserts of the Holy Land? Could an ancient Greek mechanism rusted from over two millennia on the seabed track the planets and be considered the first analogue computer? Both the Shroud of Turin and the so-called Voynich manuscript have exchanged hands and flummoxed experts since the Middle Ages. One is revered as evidence of Christ, one is written in a code that defies cryptologists. Science has managed to date these curiosities but they continue to court controversy. Can a definitive answer to their origins be determined?

# WHERE ARE THE HIDDEN TREASURES DESCRIBED IN THE COPPER SCROLL?

In 1946, at Khirbet Qumran, near the northern shore of the Dead Sea in what was then Palestine, the first of a cache of ancient scrolls was discovered in a series of caves. Known as the Dead Sea Scrolls (or Qumran Caves Scrolls), these manuscripts were written on leather parchment, tightly rolled up and stored in clay jars. The text featured large sections of the Hebrew Bible. They were a revelation, being the earliest surviving copies of entire books from the Old Testament. But, they were not the only treasures. Another scroll was found in the same caves, but it was very different in nature, being formed of rolled sheets of copper. The metal had corroded after centuries in the caves and was very brittle; the text that could be deciphered described a multitude of hidden gold and silver treasures. What riches did this Copper Scroll tell of, and could they be found?

The 14 Dead Sea Scrolls were discovered by Bedouin goatherds. The 'Copper Scroll (3Q15)', as it would be labelled, was found in 1952 by a team of archaeologists led by Frenchman Henri de Contenson, in Cave Number 3. The scroll shared the cave with scraps of parchment and papyrus manuscripts, textiles, many broken cylindrical jars, jugs and a lamp. It was in poor condition, rusted and broken in two. Both rolls rested on a natural shelf behind a large rock towards the rear of the cave's main chamber.

This position had protected the scroll from periodic collapses of the ceiling due to earthquakes. While it was found in the same location, the scroll could not be dated from the scraps of parchment and pottery nearby. It may have been stored much later.

## 'OPENING' THE SCROLL

Such was the concern for the scroll's preservation, no immediate attempt to open it was made. Instead, the scroll was put on display for three-and-a-half years, teasing its contents. Finally, a decision was made – not to unwind the scroll, which would surely have caused enormous damage, but to cut into it. The two-part scroll was taken to Manchester College of Science and Technology in England (now the University of Manchester Institute of Science and Technology), where H. Wright Baker, a professor from the Engineering Department, used a specially designed miniaturized disc saw to split the scrolls into 23 concave panels.

Tests showed the scroll was made from 99 per cent copper plus tin. It comprised very thin sheets, originally riveted together to make a scroll measuring 2.4 m (8 ft) long and 23 cm (9 in) wide. Once laid out, the panels revealed 12 columns of text that listed a great number of precious metal treasures, alongside a description of their location within ancient Palestine. The language used was a later version of Hebrew than that of the Dead Sea Scrolls, an early form of Mishnaic Hebrew (used from the mid- to late-2nd century CE). In addition, the writing in the Copper Scroll was not of the same quality: its erratic Hebrew suggested the engraver was not an experienced scribe. It was possibly copied by someone who did not speak the language, or it may have been written in a Hebrew dialect. Despite this, a Polish biblical scholar named

Józef Milik transcribed an intelligible text, which was published in 1962.

The manuscript differs notably from the text of the Dead Sea Scrolls: in particular, it lacks any biblical or religious content. Instead, it describes the hiding places of various treasures, mostly weights of gold and silver bullion, incense containers and ritual vessels. This raises the question, what is the source of these treasures?

Some experts have suggested that the loot was treasure removed from Herod's Temple in Jerusalem before the Romans attacked the city in 67CE to put down a Jewish insurgency against Roman imperialism. Another educated guess is that the treasure belonged to a Jewish sect called the Essenes, who lived at Qumran, the site of the caves. The Essenes are mentioned in the 1st-century CE writings of the Jewish historian Josephus. Perhaps the scroll lists places where the treasures were hidden for safekeeping from Roman or other hands.

Scientific dating of the metal matches this period of Roman occupation of Jerusalem, which saw the First Jewish Revolt between 66 and 70CE, followed by the burning of the city's temple. The scroll may date from a slightly later period, namely the Second Jewish Revolt, also known as the Bar-Kokhba Revolt (c.132–135CE). The Roman emperor Hadrian had ordered the city to be rebuilt as a Roman colony named Aelia Capitolina (City of the Capitoline Gods) and that a temple to Jupiter Capitolinus should be erected on the Temple Mount. This inspired a revolt led by Shimon Bar-Kokhba, which was savagely crushed. Reports say almost a thousand towns and villages were razed, around 580,000 Judean men were killed in battle, and great numbers of people died from starvation and disease. Many Judeans fled and hid in the caves

One of the 23 sections of the ancient Copper Scroll.

around Qumran. Could they have taken their religious treasures with them?

## AN ANCIENT TREASURE MAP?

One snippet of text within the Copper Scroll provides a direct link with the treasures of the Temple in Jerusalem: 'In the cave that is next to the founta[in] belonging to the House of Hakkoz, dig six cubits. [There are] six bars of gold.' Hakkoz was the name of a priestly family with a long history and a home close to the locations of many hiding places listed in the Copper Scroll. At the time of the reconstruction of the walls of Jerusalem, the family were entrusted with the treasures.

Another possible source of the hidden treasures are tithes or taxes collected in support of the Temple. While the Temple was in ruins between 70 and 132CE, these tithes may have been stored away to keep them from Roman hands.

Following their occupation, the Romans thought they had taken all of the valuable objects from Jerusalem's temples. They proudly displayed them in public processions and in the Temple of Peace back in Rome. It may be possible, however, that some valuables escaped their clutches.

Naturally, many archaeologists and treasure hunters have sought to locate the treasures listed in the Copper Scroll's panels, but the descriptions are not easy to follow. The first column of text begins with the directions: 'In the fortress which is in the Vale of Achor, forty cubits under the steps entering to the east: a money chest and it contents, of a weight of seventeen talents.' Further examples tell the reader to look 'in the salt pit that is under the steps: forty-one talents of silver. In the cave of the old washer's chamber, on the third terrace: sixty-five ingots of gold... in the gutter which is in the bottom of the (rain-water) tank', or 'in the Second Enclosure, in the underground passage that looks east', or 'in the water conduit of... the north[ern] reservoir'. Many of these landmarks, natural or human-built, no longer exist. Place names have changed or been erased, and other locations are uncertain. For example, the biblical Valley of Achor was understood to be south of Jericho, whereas later sources place it to the north-east. Kuhlith, another place named in the scroll, is thought to be hidden somewhere beneath the Samarian Desert. There are multiple interpretations that can be made from the descriptions. The Copper Scroll is no simple treasure map.

Another 'clue' reads as follows: 'Forty two talents lie under the stairs in the salt pit... Sixty five bars of gold lie on the third terrace in the cave of the old Washers House... Seventy talents of silver are enclosed in wooden vessels that are in the cistern of a burial chamber in Matia's courtyard. Fifteen cubits from the front of the eastern gates, lies a cistern. The ten talents lie in the canal of the cistern... Six silver bars are located at the sharp edge of the rock which is under the eastern wall in the cistern. The cistern's entrance is under the large paving stone threshold. Dig down four cubits in the northern corner of the pool that is east of Kohlit. There will be twenty two talents of silver coins.' While the text promises much, in practice it bewilders the modern reader.

The text lists between 61 and 64 locations in total, most of them close to the biblical town of Jericho (in today's West Bank territory). Specific measurements are given in cubits, an ancient and variable measure of length, equal to the length of the average adult forearm. These describe the distance from a landmark and the depth one would need to dig to find a treasure. Some locations include Greek letters at the end but no one has yet worked out their meaning. Were these letters in fact a specially designed code?

John Marco Allegro, the British archaeologist who brought the Copper Scroll to Manchester and supervised its opening, also provided the first English translation of the text, two years before Józef Milik's approved version. Allegro used his transcription as a guide to explore Israel and Jordan and dig at several sites, but he was unsuccessful in his search for the scroll's treasures. Perhaps he chose the wrong places, or the treasure had been looted long ago.

## AN ANCIENT TWO-STEP VERIFICATION METHOD?

A tantalizing detail in the scroll's text is the description of the 64th treasure: 'a duplicate of this document and an explanation and their measurements and a precise reckoning of everything, one by one'. It may be that this second, hidden scroll is needed to unlock the secrets of the first. This could even be a Catch-22 situation, where the second scroll is not retrievable without knowledge of its contents secreted in the first scroll.

The scroll lists more than 4,600 talents of precious metal, a talent being a Greek or Roman weight equivalent to between 32 kg (71 lb) and 59 kg (130lb). Overall, the weight in gold and silver may be between 52 and 158 tonnes. The value of the treasure described in the Copper Scroll has been estimated at one billion dollars.

Another question asked by archaeologists and other scholars is why was the scroll etched on copper? Such a scroll would have been expensive to produce, requiring one or maybe more craftspeople sufficiently skilled with a hammer and chisel to carefully incise the letters in to the thin sheets of metal. Presumably, copper was chosen because it was thought to be long lasting. Whoever was responsible for creating and hiding it clearly thought the treasure it described would need to be hidden for generations.

The pieces of the Copper Scroll are now on display at the Jordan Museum in the country's capital, Amman. Improved restoration techniques, including more precise photography, X-rays and cleaning, have aided the reading of the text through the corroded copper. Despite the efforts of scientists, biblical experts, archaeologists and treasure hunters over decades, none of the described fortune has so far been unearthed. Has the treasure trove already been looted, or did it even exist in the first place? There is no doubt the search will go on when further exploration is allowed in the region. Or, perhaps, history will repeat itself and a Bedouin goatherd will accidentally come across further riches from antiquity – maybe another scroll or the long-lost treasures themselves. Until then, the Copper Scroll continues to tease rich rewards in the sands beside the Dead Sea.

# WAS THE ANTIKYTHERA MECHANISM AN ANCIENT COMPUTER?

A rusted, geared device from long ago, dredged up from the seabed near the tiny Greek island of Antikythera, has puzzled experts for

120 years. It was the most technologically advanced device ever seen from the ancient world, but what was its purpose: ancient computer, astronomical clock, or something else? The complexity of the device inspired moviemakers to design a similar item as the time-twisting treasure sought in the 2023 film *Indiana Jones and the Dial of Destiny*. After centuries of corrosion was cleared away and fresh methods of investigation became available, new theories about what this mechanism was capable of have come to light and astonished experts.

In 1900, while diving 45 m (148 ft) deep for sponges in the waters off Antikythera, Elias Stadiatis came across something that made him almost jump out of his heavy canvas diving suit. He described the sight as a 'heap of dead naked people'. In fact, Stadiatis had found an ancient shipwreck with a cargo including several bronze and marble statues. It also included wine jars, glassware, pottery, silver coins and plates. His discovery launched the first major underwater archaeological dig in history.

Among the treasures brought to the surface was a lump of corroded metal, the size of a shoebox. All the artefacts found aboard the wreck were brought to the National Archaeological Museum in Athens for study, but the rusted block went largely ignored for two years while staff concentrated on more recognizable treasures, like the statues. Meanwhile, the rusted object broke apart into three pieces.

## PREDICTING PLANETARY MOVEMENTS

The German philologist Albert Rehm was one of the first to examine it, between 1905 and 1906. He saw that it contained cogs and gearwheels and suggested it could be an astronomical clock of some kind. He found several figures inscribed in the device that matched those used in earlier Babylonian astronomical measurements (Babylon, in today's southern Iraq, was at its height by around 1850BCE). The number 19, for example, could have been a reference to the 19-year 'Metonic cycle', which describes the motion of the Moon against the stars. The figure 223 may have referenced the number of lunar months in a Babylonian eclipse-prediction cycle. Efforts to decipher the workings of the mechanism continued for decades, until a major breakthrough came in 1974, when X-ray technology was used to probe its secrets.

The device was thought to have measured 34 cm (13 in) tall when intact. It contained over 30 gearwheels; the largest gear was about 13 cm (5 in) in diameter and once had 223 teeth. The smallest was 8 mm in diameter with 15 teeth, each just 1 mm long. Some parts were covered with astronomical, mathematical and mechanical inscriptions, presumably instructions on the use and interpretation of the mechanism. With a two-dimensional map of the machine's workings, experts were able to confirm that the gears could calculate the average position of the Moon on any specific date. Its designers had even improved on the Babylonian calculations for planetary cycles.

Using the information gathered by X-ray examinations, engineers built a working replica of the Antikythera mechanism. Cast in brass rather than the original bronze, the mechanism was housed in a wooden container. On the front were two dials: one displaying the days of the year, based on the Egyptian calendar, the other the signs of the zodiac. Metal hands pointed to the positions of the Sun, Moon and five classical planets (Mercury, Venus, Mars, Jupiter and Saturn). By turning a knob on the side of the mechanism, users could set it to a given date and discover the location of the Sun and five planets on that day.

Further X-ray probes (in three dimensions by 2005) uncovered much more text inscribed inside the rear door of the device's housing. This was, effectively, a user manual. Further refinements in the design have been tested with 3-D computer models. These developments showed that the Antikythera mechanism was a revolutionary device far beyond anything else discovered from the ancient world. But when and where was it from, and who built it?

## DATING AN ANCIENT MECHANICAL MARVEL

The shipwreck had been dated to between 60 and 70BCE, and was first thought to have been a Roman vessel carrying plunder from

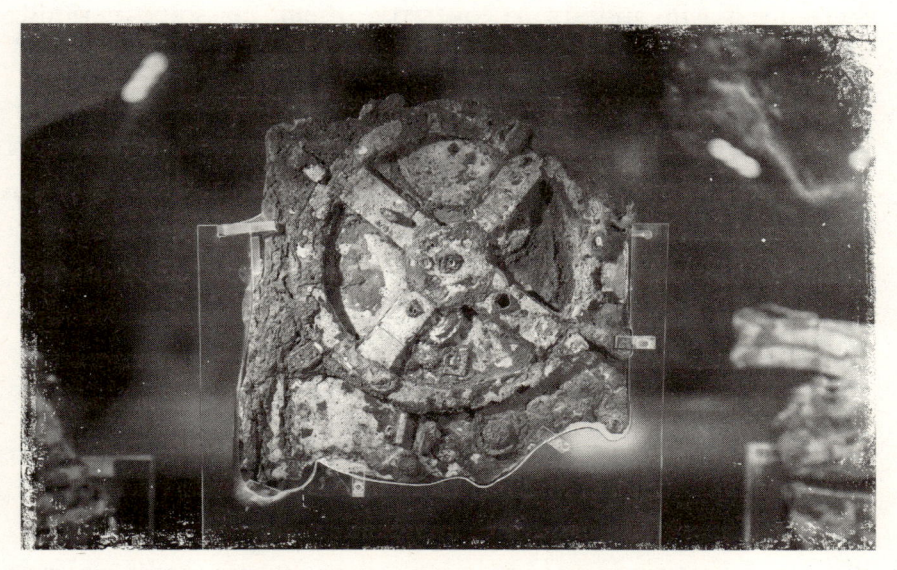

The largest fragment of the Antikythera mechanism, Athens National Archaeological Museum, Greece.

Greece to Rome. It is now understood to have been a trading vessel. The Antikythera mechanism had to be older than the shipwreck and has since been dated to around 200BCE. There are no records to suggest sophisticated engineering like that used in the device existed at the time, either in ancient Greece or anywhere else in the world. No earlier geared device has ever been found. Clockwork devices did not appear in western Europe until centuries later, during the Middle Ages.

The ancient Greeks observed the heavens without the aid of telescopes, mapping the movements of five planets among the 'fixed stars'. They described the planets as 'wanderers', but did not know what they were or why their paths would sometimes follow the direction of the Sun, pause, then switch direction (move in retrograde) for a period. We now know that the planetary routes appear this way from Earth because they orbit the Sun, not Earth, therefore Earth appears to 'overtake' them for some periods. Predicting the positions of these wanderers was very difficult for early astronomers.

The ship carrying the Antikythera device also contained pottery identified as having been manufactured on the island of Rhodes. Rhodes had become a busy trading port in the 1st century BCE, and a known centre for astronomy and mechanical engineering. This prompted experts to claim that the mechanism originated there too. The island was home to the astronomer Hipparchus, who was active during the period the mechanism was crafted (he is thought to have died after 127BCE). Hipparchus developed a theory for the motion of the Moon, which was used in the device.

Later, the Stoic philosopher Posidonius set up a school on Rhodes, following Hipparchus's teachings. Reports from Cicero, the 1st-century BCE Roman consul, claimed that Posidonius had made an instrument 'which at each revolution reproduces the same motions of the Sun, the Moon and the five planets that take place in the heavens every day and night'. This sounds remarkably like the Antikythera mechanism. Cicero also wrote of a similar device built by the famous Greek mathematician and inventor Archimedes in 212BCE, although this was supposedly stolen by a Roman general named Marcellus.

The Antikythera mechanism is a great advance on any other invention from the 1st or 2nd century BCE, which suggests there must have been prototypes and similar machines in production that have either not survived or are still to be discovered. Similar devices may have been melted down for their valuable bronze. A big question is why there do not appear to have been any further refinements of this technology in ancient Greece?

It would be centuries before such sophisticated machinery reappeared. A geared calendar attached to a sundial was in operation in the Byzantine Empire, but that was at least 600 years later. Various mechanical devices were tested in 9th-century Baghdad. In 11th-century China, the scientist Su Sing developed a mechanical clock tower that also marked the position of planets and stars.

These later devices do not necessarily show a continuance of mechanical design from the Antikythera mechanism. The astronomical clock found in a wreck in the Aegean Sea is, so far, a one-off. This single artefact proves that the astronomers and engineers of ancient Greece were capable of creating wonders – even something tentatively described as the world's first analogue computer.

# IS THE SHROUD OF TURIN A MIRACLE OR A HOAX?

When it was first seen in public in the mid-14th century, the holy shroud was venerated as a miraculous image of Jesus Christ. Now housed in Turin, Italy, the most famous Christian relic of all continues to hold a sway over believers. But is this cloth an imprint of Christ after his death or is it a medieval fake? Where did it come from and, if it was fashioned by human hand, who was responsible?

Christian relics were not of much interest in the first centuries following the death of Christ. There are no mentions of pieces of the cross, thorns or cloaks being prized and venerated. That changed in the 4th century when Constantine, the first Roman emperor to convert to Christianity, looked east and sent his mother, Helena (later St Helena), to visit the holiest sites in Jerusalem and Bethlehem in 326. Helena sought out the Cave of the Nativity, the Holy Sepulchre (believed to be the site of Jesus's death, burial and resurrection), and the site of Christ's supposed ascension on the Mount of Olives. During her quest, Helena claimed to have found Christ's tomb and the cross that bore Jesus. Proof that this was the 'True Cross' supposedly came when it restored a dead man to life before her eyes. The market for relics was born.

## EARLY RELICS OF CHRIST

The Shroud of Turin is not the first miraculous image of Christ to have been shared. The 'first icon' of Jesus is recorded as appearing in the 4th century. The Mandylion (Greek for towel) was supposed to have recorded the image of Christ after he used it to wipe his face. According to one legend, it was delivered to King Abgar of Osroene in his capital Edessa (in modern-day Syria) by an emissary from Jesus, to help the king recover from illness. In another version of the story, the image was painted, with the artist able to capture Jesus's likeness through miraculous means.

The Mandylion was taken to Constantinople by the Byzantine army in 944, where it remained until the knights of the Fourth Crusade sacked the city in 1204 and removed the icon. It is thought to have then passed into the hands of King Louis IX of France and been stored in the royal chapel of Sainte-Chapelle in Paris, until it disappeared centuries later during the French Revolution. (It has been suggested that this image was the Shroud of Turin but folded, so that only the face of Christ was seen.)

The first report of the Shroud of Turin dates back to 1354, when the French knight Geoffroi de Charny displayed it in a small church in the hamlet of Lirey in north-central France. In 1453, his granddaughter, Margaret de Charny, sold the shroud to the royal House of Savoy in exchange for two castles. (She was excommunicated for doing so.) While in the possession of the Savoyards, the shroud suffered fire and water damage that is still visible today. It was relocated to its final home in the Cathedral of Saint John the Baptist (San Giovanni Battista) in Turin, Italy, in 1578, after the House of Savoy claimed Turin as its capital.

The shroud was first photographed in 1898 by an Italian lawyer and amateur photographer named Secondo Pia, who discovered the images on the linen were much clearer on his negative plates. The original shroud is now guarded by security cameras, in an airtight frame behind bulletproof glass, and only rarely displayed in public, drawing millions of pilgrims. A replica can be seen in the Museum of the Shroud in Turin.

The shroud is a rectangle of linen measuring 4.3 m (14 ft) long and 1.1 m (3.5 ft) wide. It is marked with pale brown images that seem to be the result of an imprint of a naked male figure who was around 1.7 m (5 ft 7 in) tall and lying down at rest. One half shows the figure's front, his hands covering his groin, and the other his back. The figure is gaunt, long-haired and bearded, and bears the marks of injury consistent with Biblical stories that Jesus was whipped, made to wear a crown of thorns that pierced his scalp, then crucified with nails hammered into his hands and feet.

What of the shroud's provenance? Is there anything in its history that links it directly with the death of Christ? The New Testament gospels do refer to Jesus's body being wrapped in a linen shroud that was found later by Simon Peter, discarded in Christ's

The shroud on display in Turin, Italy, in 2015.

tomb after the resurrection. However, there is no record of a burial garment with an image of Jesus on it prior to the shroud coming into the hands of Geoffroi de Charny. Nor is there any mention of it being seen or possessed, which seems odd for a relic of such consequence.

## RELIGION AND SCIENCE QUESTION THE SHROUD

Doubts were raised very early on after the shroud appeared and news of its existence spread. It was condemned as a fake around 1389 by Pierre d'Arcis, Bishop of Troyes in north-central France, who described it as 'cunningly painted, the truth being attested by the artist who painted it'. He also claimed the dean of the church in Lirey was aware that it was fake but continued to display it in order to raise funds. Clement VII, the Avignon-based Roman Catholic 'antipope' at the time, sanctioned the shroud's display but ordered the Church to 'say aloud, to put an end to all fraud, that the aforementioned representation is not the true Shroud of Our Lord Jesus Christ, but a painting or panel made to represent or imitate the Shroud'. In 1506, Pope Julius II reversed this command and accepted it as a true representation of Christ.

It is interesting to note that while popes may have become convinced of the shroud's authenticity over time, much earlier in 1418, while keeping the shroud safe at his castle, Margaret de Charny's husband wrote a receipt for the shroud that openly acknowledged it was not Jesus's authentic burial cloth.

Many attempts have been made to verify or deny the origin of the shroud over the last century. In 1978, the American chemist Walter McCrone (known as the 'father of modern microscopy') removed a sample using adhesive tape. He claimed the images on the cloth had been painted with a dilute solution of red ochre and that the 'bloodstains' were a vermillion pigment. In 1988, the Vatican provided three different laboratories with small squares of the shroud's cloth for tests using carbon-dating methods. All three laboratories produced results that dated the cloth to between 1260 and 1390 – matching the timing of its first presentation by Geoffroi de Charny.

In 2002, a 1st-century CE burial shroud was found in Jerusalem. Comparisons between this and the Shroud of Turin showed that the relic does not match the materials of the time. The herringbone weave in the cloth was a medieval design that would not have been used during Jesus's day.

So, if it was not an imprint of a dead man and his wounds, how was the shroud image made? Walter McCrone found that a similar

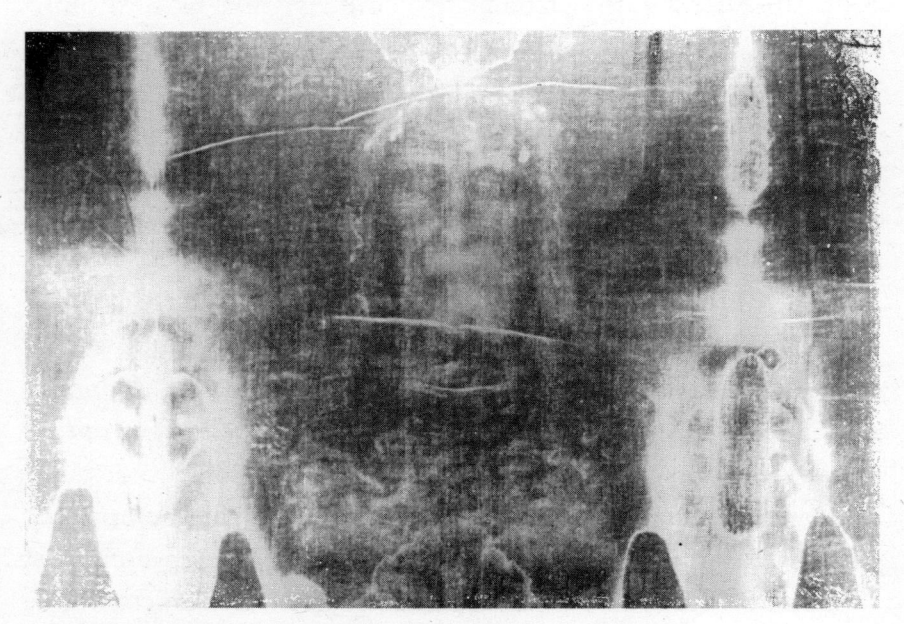

A face revealed in a photo negative of the shroud.

effect could have been created using a medieval painting method called *grisaille*, using tempura on linen. In 2009 Luigi Garlaschelli, a professor of organic chemistry at the University of Pavia, Italy, used methods from the Middle Ages to reproduce the visual effect of the shroud, by covering a volunteer with cloth and rubbing the material with a pigment containing traces of acid, before artificially aging the cloth by heating and washing it. It seems perfectly possible that a talented 14th-century artist could have been employed to leave a convincing image of Christ on cloth.

While four churches in France and three in Italy currently lay claim to the burial cloth of Jesus, none has been held in as much awe as the one in Turin. Despite historic declarations and scientific proof asserting that the shroud did not wrap the body of Christ, it continues to be venerated and viewed as genuine by many Christians. Some argue that the medieval dating shows only that the shroud was repaired during that period, or that samples were contaminated. The Catholic Church appears to sit on the fence in regard to a verdict. In 1998, Pope John Paul II said of the matter, 'Since it is not a matter of faith, the Church has no specific competence to pronounce on these questions. She entrusts to scientists the task of continuing to investigate, so that satisfactory answers may be found to the questions connected with this Sheet.'

In 2020, during the COVID-19 pandemic, Cesare Nosiglia, Archbishop of Turin, permitted an online stream of the shroud to offer some consolation to people who were bereaved or distressed by the devastating events. Attempts are still being made today to prove the cloth touched the body of Christ. It has an emotive power that attracts both believers and sceptics. Whether it is a relic of Christ or a relic of medieval ingenuity, the Shroud of Turin is certainly a fascinating historical artefact.

# CAN THE VOYNICH MANUSCRIPT CODE BE CRACKED?

The Voynich Manuscript has confounded many experts and amateur sleuths since it was revealed to the world in the early 20th century. This vellum manuscript, possibly dating from the 15th century, is handwritten in a language that has defied linguists and cryptologists. It contains images of exotic plants that look familiar yet cannot be identified for certain, and features images of naked bathing women and bizarre contraptions, which may or may not be offering health treatments. Does this strange manuscript hide alchemical secrets from the distant past? Or is it simply a collection of gibberish, or even an elaborate medieval hoax?

This single volume is named after the book dealer who first raised interest in its coded contents. Wilfrid Voynich was born in Lithuania, then part of the Russian Empire, in 1865. The son of a Polish-Lithuanian noble family, Voynich graduated from university with a degree in chemistry. He drifted into politics, joining groups aiming to free Poland from Russian rule. In 1885, he was arrested for his involvement in revolutionary activities and imprisoned in Warsaw Citadel. Around 1890, Voynich escaped and fled to London under an assumed name. From here, he began smuggling anti-tsarist books back into eastern Europe. Eventually, Voynich gave up on revolution and set up an antiquarian book business, opening a store in central London's Soho Square in 1898.

Voynich proved a shrewd negotiator and soon gathered an impressive catalogue of titles. In 1912, he came into the possession of a manuscript that would beguile generations of bibliophiles. Voynich was vague about where he found it, claiming it was part of a collection of illuminated manuscripts gathered in a chest in an ancient castle in southern Europe. As Voynich described it, 'My attention was especially drawn by one volume. It was such an ugly duckling compared with the others that my interest was aroused at once. I found that it was entirely written in cipher. Even a necessarily brief examination of the vellum upon which it was written, the calligraphy, the drawings and the pigment suggested to me as the date of its origin the latter part of the thirteenth century.'

The manuscript is in a small quarto format with pages measuring 23 cm by 15 cm (9 in by 6 in) on average. It contains 240 pages in total, with at least eight missing. Some pages are gate-folded and can therefore be extended beyond the standard page size. Most of the pages feature drawings tinted with inks. The first section covers botanical subjects, with images of 113 unidentified plants, showing their flowers, leaves and roots. The second section covers the zodiac and astronomical subjects, and also has images of nude women emerging from tubes. More naked, possibly pregnant, women feature in the third section; these figures are illustrated in baths of green liquid that are connected with tubing. Finally, there is a series of nine circular images filled with stars, plant-like parts and pipes, images of plants in jars, and what is presumed to be a key to the book's contents.

While the images, drawn in an amateurish hand, were intriguing, it was the accompanying text that captivated those seeking to understand the manuscript. Now described as 'Voynichese', the writing at first appears to be an archaic language similar to Latin.

Indeed, some letters are familiar, some match numerals, and some are more florid, but others do not match any known language. Several characters are repeated with variations, or are part of compound characters. Studies of the text have struggled to specify exactly how many different symbols are used in it: estimates range between 23 and 40.

Having secured the manuscript, Voynich then tried to trace its origin. His first thought was that it was the work of the 13th-century English philosopher and Franciscan friar Roger Bacon (c.1219–c.1292). This was a credible choice: Bacon, also known by the name 'Doctor Mirabilis', was an inventive scholar who pioneered scientific experimentation rather than presuming that all answers lie in faith. His studies and published works covered subjects including optics, linguistics, astrology and alchemy.

Voynich claimed that he had initially overlooked a letter attached to the front of the manuscript that would have helped him in his research. This letter, dated 19 August 1665 or 1666, was written by a Joannes Marcus Marci of Cronland, Prague, and sent to an Athanasius, a 'Reverend and Distinguished Sir, Father in Christ'.

## ATTEMPTS TO DECODE 'VOYNICHESE'

Athanasius turned out to be Athanasius Kircher, a German Jesuit scholar from the prestigious Collegio Romano in Rome, who claimed to have deciphered Egyptian hieroglyphs. The letter explained that the (unnamed) owner of the manuscript had previously sent Kircher samples, hoping that he might be able to decode it. Now that the manuscript owner had died, his friend, Joannes Marcus Marci, was sending Kircher the full manuscript.

A translation of Marci's accompanying letter read: 'The former owner of this book asked your opinion by letter, copying and sending you a portion of the book from which he believed you would be able to read the remainder, but he at that time refused to send the book itself. To its deciphering he devoted unflagging toil, as is apparent from attempts of his which I send you herewith, and he relinquished hope only with his life. But his toil was in vain, for such Sphinxes as these obey no one but their master, Kircher. Accept now this token, such as it is and long overdue though it be, of my affection for you, and burst through its bars, if there are any, with your wonted success.'

Kircher's claim that he had cracked the code of Egyptian hieroglyphics would prove to be false. Kircher saw them as symbols, with each image representing an idea. (The discovery of the Rosetta Stone in 1799 would lead to the revelation that hieroglyphs instead represented syllables.) Whether or not Kircher received the Voynich Manuscript and worked on a decryption is unknown, as there is no evidence that he even attempted it. Perhaps he did, and it was beyond his abilities.

Research by Voynich and later investigators identified the owner described in Joannes Marcus Marci's letter as Georg Baresch, a 17th-century alchemist from Prague. It was Baresch who initially contacted Athanasius Kircher requesting his help to decrypt the volume.

Marci's letter claimed the manuscript had once been the property of the Holy Roman Emperor Rudolf II, who paid 600 ducats for it on the understanding it was the work of 'Roger Bacon, the Englishman'. This conveniently supported Voynich's claim that the book had been written by 'Doctor Mirabilis', but also raised the question of who sold it to Emperor Rudolf. Once again Voynich had an answer, namely John Dee.

Another intriguing figure from English history, John Dee (1527–c.1608) was a mathematician, astrologer and alchemist with a fascination for the occult. After dodging an accusation of treason, Dee found work as an astrological and scientific advisor to Queen Elizabeth I. He also built up one of the largest private libraries in England. Thus it seemed plausible that Dee might be the kind of individual who would acquire a volume like the Voynich Manuscript.

With World War I on the horizon, Voynich left London in 1914 and sailed to the United States, where he opened a new bookshop in New York City. There, he began soliciting interest in the Voynich Manuscript by sending photostatic copies of the most interesting pages to various experts on historical writing and Roger Bacon, as well as cryptographers.

William Newbold, professor of philosophy at the University of Pennsylvania, was one of the first to take up the challenge presented by this strange codex. Newbold claimed to have unlocked its code after seeing just three pages supplied from the manuscript. Rather than trying to decrypt the book's coded text, Newbold examined the pages under a microscope and spied tiny markings around the words, which he identified as being based on ancient Greek shorthand. He also claimed that one grouped image of stars was a depiction of the Andromeda Galaxy (the closest major galaxy to our Milky Way).

Newbold agreed that Roger Bacon was the author of the book, but his conclusions meant that the 13th-century friar must have had access to both a microscope and telescope, 300 years before their known invention. In addition, the code that Bacon supposedly developed was far in advance of any encryption systems used during his time. As for the naked nymphs, Newbold understood these as human souls drawn to Earth through sexual intercourse. He identified certain images as microscopic views of sperm and ova. Newbold was not able to decrypt the entire manuscript. After a short illness, he died in 1926.

When Newbold's workings were published posthumously they were found to be lacking. In his 1931 review of the work, Professor John Mathews Manly of the University of Chicago wrote, 'In my opinion, the Newbold claims are entirely baseless and should be definitely and absolutely rejected.' He pointed out that the 'Greek shorthand' scrawls Newbold found on the pages through a microscope were not veiled text, but merely areas where the ink had bled into fine flaws in the ancient vellum.

Although translations of the text were proving problematic, further clues to the manuscript's history were emerging. While preparing photostats of the manuscript for Newbold, Voynich

Examination of the Voynich Manuscript under magnification.

had noticed a faint signature on an underexposed copy of the first page. Treatment with chemicals revealed the name 'Jacob de Tepenecz'.

De Tepenecz, born Jacobus Sinapius, was a Bohemian scientist who became wealthy through the invention of an alchemical remedy: essentially, he was an early snake-oil salesman. Sinapius became pharmacist and keeper of the royal gardens for Emperor Rudolf II (also King of Bohemia), who honoured him with the noble name 'de Tepenecz' in 1608. With de Tepenecz's signature, Voynich had proof that the manuscript was changing hands in the early 17th century.

Despite evidence of the book's pedigree, Voynich failed to find a buyer for his bizarre manuscript with its price tag of $160,000 (about $2.8 million in today's value). In 1930, Voynich died of lung cancer, aged 64. Although his prized manuscript remained undeciphered and unsold, interest in decoding its contents did not wane.

In 1943, an American lawyer, Joseph Martin Feely, published the book *Roger Bacon's Cipher: The Right Key Found*, in which he claimed Bacon had used an abbreviated version of medieval Latin as a code. Feely came to his conclusions without full access to the manuscript. His theories have also been discredited.


## NO HIDDEN MESSAGE?

The US military codebreaker (and codemaker) William F. Friedman was considered one of the greatest cryptologists of the 20th century, having deciphered the Japanese Code Purple during World War II. Despite his skill, he found the Voynich Manuscript's text impossible to unravel and suggested it might be an invented language rather than a code. Later researchers claimed the text had roots in Hebrew, medieval Turkish and even Tibetan.

Robert S. Brumbaugh, a professor of classical and medieval philosophy at Yale University, published several articles recording his efforts to fathom the book's secrets through the 1970s. He believed that the symbols in the manuscript were based on a system, with each symbol representing a number that could then be switched to a letter of the alphabet. Unfortunately, the text that resulted from this two-step method made little or no sense whatsoever. Ultimately, Brumbaugh thought the manuscript had 'no hidden message and all that there is is simply text'. In his view the manuscript was deliberate nonsense, but with just enough detail to keep codebreakers interested, or to convince a wealthy patron, such as Emperor Rudolf II, to part with his money.

The manuscript not only suffers for its unintelligible coding but also for an apparent lack of routine grammar. Most of the words comprise four or five letters – there are none with one or two letters, or ten or more. There are also no double letters, no obvious punctuation, and many strings of symbols appear multiple times in succession. According to experts the text just doesn't act like natural language. It has been suggested that meaningful text is hidden among gibberish, but this begs the question of how to separate the two. The situation is further complicated by the possibility raised by experts that more than one person had a hand in the text; up to 12 authors have been posited as being responsible for the handwriting.

The manuscript's botanical images have also proved to be near unfathomable. It has been assumed that they are herbal plants with the text describing their use in remedies – the problem is, identifying the plants has been near impossible. Flower heads seem to be grafted on to the stems, leaves and roots of other plants. Hugh O'Neill, an eminent botanist at the Catholic University of America, felt the drawings were deliberately obtuse, although he did tentatively suggest that one could be the common sunflower and another a form of capsicum. If O'Neill was correct, it would mean the manuscript must have been produced after 1493, because Christopher Columbus introduced these plants to Europe after his second voyage to the New World.

The pages featuring naked women in and out of baths give the impression they are describing medical procedures. While it's hard to tell if the women are pregnant or simply have rounded bellies, these activities could be treatments to aid childbirth or even prevent it. The illustrations appear somewhat bizarre to a modern reader: the women emerge from single and communal baths, or a kind of ovarian tubing, and reach towards further organic shapes that are alien or plantlike in form. The gynaecological subject matter (and explicit images) may have been the reason the author self-censored using code.

Less troubling are the astronomical diagrams. These are made up of a series of circles, most with the Sun at the centre and stars dotted about. There are 12 circular diagrams in all, representing the signs of the zodiac, and it's notable that Aries and Taurus are repeated. The presumption is that these pages offer some manner of astrological advice.

Overall, the combination of text and imagery in the Voynich Manuscript suggests something slightly magical, and the lack of rational content does suggest alternative conclusions about the material. Perhaps the book represents the thoughts and feelings of someone with a psychiatric disorder, who is using quill and paper to make sense of the world as they see it. Alternatively, could its

Exotic, unidentified plant illustration from the Voynich Manuscript.

creator be trying to translate information that they believe they have received from an otherworldly source? John Dee, Voynich's candidate for the author, was one of many people known for their serious attempts to conjure up spirits.

## ONE, POSSIBLY TWO, CHARLATANS

A name that often arises when discussing John Dee is that of the notorious occultist Edward Kelley (1555–c.1597), a lawyer who was found guilty of forgery and had his ears cropped in punishment. He was later charged with digging up corpses and used a pseudonym to escape justice. In 1582, Kelley convinced Dee that he could help him with his experiments into the paranormal and to induce visions of angels. As a forger and a charlatan, could Kelley have transcribed the Voynich Manuscript, with or without Dee's involvement, and then convinced Emperor Rudolf of its worth? The manuscript could have been a deliberate attempt to pass off nonsense as a coded bible of alchemical procedures. If it is a forgery, then it could also have been produced in more recent history, perhaps by the man who seemed to be most eager to profit from it – Wilfrid Voynich.

Voynich was not entirely honourable in his dealings. In 1916 he was found guilty in court of stealing a library book from Lincoln Cathedral. He was also reported to have fleeced a monastery out of their valuable manuscripts by convincing them more modern manuals were a better investment. Hints at possible deception by Voynich include the convenient late appearance of de Tepenecz's signature. Voynich could converse (poorly) in several languages and may have sourced some ancient vellum on which to write unintelligible text. It must be noted, though, that sourcing

240 pages' worth of ancient vellum to write upon would be a challenge.

Following Wilfrid Voynich's death, the ancient castle in southern Europe where he found the manuscript was identified as Villa Madragone, a former Jesuit college in Frascati, Italy. Apparently, the Jesuits sold off part of their collection of rare manuscripts to help fund restoration work. The manuscript passed from Voynich's widow, Ethel, to her friend Anne Nill, who sold it for US$24,500 (£18,300) to a New York book dealer named Hans Kraus. Kraus failed to profit from it and in 1969 he donated it to the Beinecke Rare Book and Manuscript Library at Yale University. It has remained there ever since, alongside a Shakespeare First Folio and a Gutenberg Bible.

In 2009, the Voynich Manuscript finally underwent carbon-dating. The results showed that it was written on calfskin dating from between 1404 and 1438 and the paint used for the illustrations came from a similar period. However, this does not confirm that the text was actually written or the illustrations made during that time period.

In a recent twist in this story, the Spanish publisher Siloe produced 898 exact replicas of the manuscript in 2017, costing €8,000 (£6,600) each. A high-resolution scan of the volume is available online and a community of manuscript detectives continues to share their insights and theories. We may never know the truth behind the origin of the Voynich Manuscript or fully understand its strange text but it has never been easier for amateur sleuths to try to decode it. Perhaps this ongoing community effort to find meaning in a medieval manuscript is what it is about. A solution may be disappointing compared to conjecture.

# CHAPTER 4
# LOST IN TIME

Archaeologists and historians work like detectives, scouring sites and documents for clues that may unravel ancient mysteries, possibly even crimes. Perhaps the most difficult puzzles to solve are those that involve the missing. The fate of the Neanderthals is one of the oldest of such riddles. Were they wiped out by war with *Homo sapiens*, or by competition and disease, and how does their legacy live on? Last seen marching through Britain in the 2nd century CE, Rome's Ninth Legion apparently vanished. What force annihilated this professional and highly disciplined army?

What of the Ark of the Covenant and the Holy Grail – sacred artefacts that have inspired devotion and literary quests? What proof do we have of their existence and, if they survive, in which corner of the world could they be hidden? Was the ancient Egyptian boy-king Tutankhamun murdered, and where was his successor, the famously alluring Cleopatra entombed? Forensic science and even underwater archaeology are bringing us closer than ever to resolving these and more classical conundrums.

# WHY DID THE NEANDERTHALS DIE OUT?

For decades *Homo neanderthalensis* was imagined as the archetypal caveman: thick of brow, hunched over, grunting and primitive. In recent years this picture has been heavily revised, and we now know that while Neanderthals were stockier than modern humans (*Homo sapiens*), they had similar capacities. DNA studies have revealed interspecies sex took place about 50,000 years ago, and that there is a little Neanderthal in all humans whose ancestral group developed outside Africa. If Neanderthals had comparable skills to, and lived alongside, *Homo sapiens*, why did they come to a dead end?

Neanderthals are our closest ancient human relatives; we shared a common ancestor at some time between 600,000 and 800,000 years ago. They were the first human species to permanently make Europe their home and since the early 19th century their remains have been discovered across Europe, from the British Isles to Siberia. Their bones have been dated from 430,000 years to 30,000 years ago, which means they existed for around 200,000 years longer than *Homo sapiens* have so far.

Around 45,000 years ago, *Homo sapiens* found their way from Africa to Europe, a journey they had attempted, unsuccessfully, at least once before. They certainly encountered *Homo neanderthalensis*, but there is no evidence of violence between the species – just the opposite. The publication of the Neanderthal genome in 2010 proved that they interbred and that we share 99 per cent of our DNA with Neanderthals.

The first Neanderthal bone fragments were discovered in Belgium in 1829, but it was not until further finds in 1856 that palaeontologists realized they had found the first-ever fossils of early humans. The location of the bones, in a cave in the Neander Valley in Germany, led to the Irish geologist William King naming the species *Homo neanderthalensis*, or 'Human from the Neander Valley'. Bone fossils found before this were then retrospectively identified as Neanderthal.

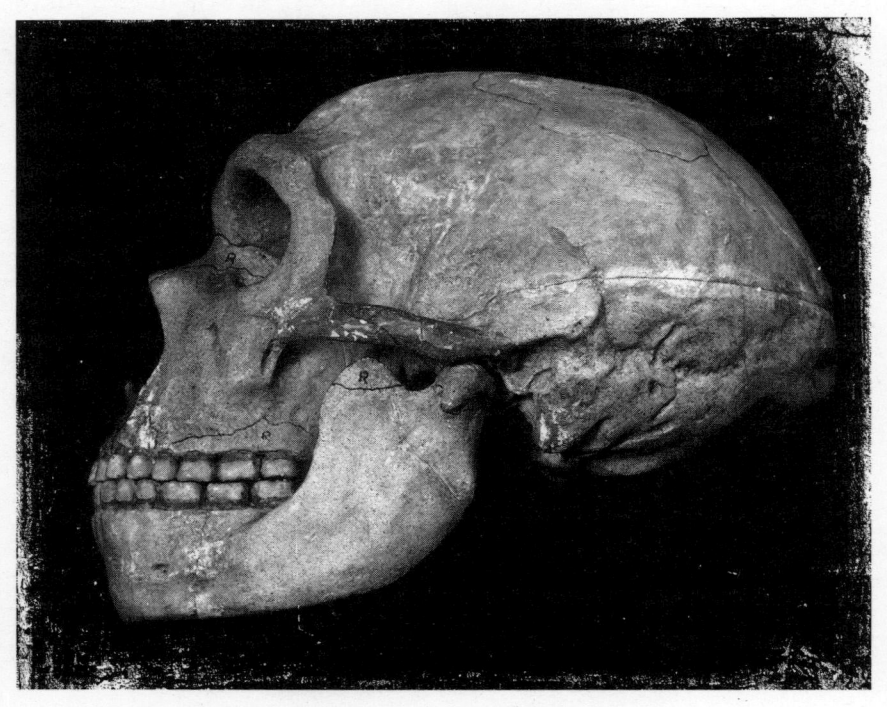

Neanderthal skull found at Chapelle-aux-Saints, France.

## THE NEANDERTHAL 'OLD MAN'

In 1908, an almost complete male skeleton was found in La Chapelle-aux-Saints, central France. His skull featured a low forehead and prominent brow, which was regarded as ape-like. The individual was old and suffered from an arthritic condition. In part due to his deformed bones, the skeleton was reconstructed by the French palaeontologist and geologist Pierre-Marcellin Boule as a bent-over primitive. It would take a long time and much new evidence for the perception of the Neanderthal as a stooping, ape-like subhuman to be supplanted.

Just how different were Neanderthals to the 'caveman' concept? While they did rest in caves, Neanderthals also built shelters. In two sites in France, archaeologists found holes in the ground where posts were likely to have been driven in to support twigs or leather skins and form a fence or tent. Charcoal and bones from 60,000 years ago show that Neanderthals also controlled fire and cooked meals. Their diet included meat (notably deer and larger mammals), marine mammals (such as seals and scavenged dolphin carcasses), fish, shellfish, nuts, seeds, mushrooms and tubers. Some of their plant intake may have even been for medicinal purposes.

In 2018, researchers at the Monrepos Archaeological Research Center in Neuwied, Germany, studied the puncture marks on ancient animal bones and concluded that Neanderthals used close-range hunting techniques. They must have been able to form teams and plan to hunt large prey such as bison, rhinos and mammoths. This would have involved stalking herds and steering them towards ambushes. For this and more, they also made tools. They could chip flint into useful knives, axes and points that they attached to wooden spears. They may have even mixed a type of tar glue by burning the bark from birch trees.

Neanderthals also appear to have cared for weaker and older individuals. The skeleton found in La Chapelle-aux-Saints, France in 1908, nicknamed 'Old Man', was almost toothless so he may have needed his food to be ground or mashed in order to digest it. According to France's National Center for Scientific Research, the elderly Neanderthal was unlikely to have survived in this condition for long on his own, and therefore may have had help. Elsewhere, the remains of a 50,000-year-old, one-armed and partly deaf adult male were unearthed in Shanidar Cave, northern Iraq, in 1957. This severely wounded Neanderthal must also have had support to reach his forties.

## A LIFE BEYOND SURVIVAL?

Another intriguing question around these early humans is their capacity for cultural practices or communal behaviour. The remains of some Neanderthals appear to have been buried. While this may have been to discourage scavenging animals, it may also have been part of a deliberate ritual, suggesting that Neanderthals honoured individuals. A 70,000-year-old Neanderthal grave discovered in Teshik-Tash, Uzbekistan, contained a nine-year-old boy placed beside ibex horns. Evidence of pollen grains in a Neanderthal grave in Iraq's Shanidar Cave at first suggested that shamanistic ceremonies took place, or that bodies were interred with flowers, although this is now disputed.

It is thought that Neanderthals did decorate themselves, perhaps with pigments. They may have caught birds for both food and the feathers they supplied for adornment. The talons of large birds of prey appear to have been put aside for decorative purposes. In two caves in Spain, the presence of perforated and painted shells dating from 50,000 years ago led experts to submit that Neanderthals wore them as jewellery, and that they invented strings to thread them. Three-ply cords found with Neanderthal remains suggest that they were capable of making thread from bark fibres found inside trees. They are likely to have worn clothes of some kind, and could have used their teeth to chew and soften animal skins.

Whether Neanderthals were capable of art is debatable, but it appears they did make deliberate marks. In Gotham's Cave in Gibraltar, 39,000-year-old scratches can be seen on the cave floor, forming a hashtag-type pattern. This design may have had symbolic meaning, or it could simply have been scored into the rock out of boredom. What has been described as a bone flute was found at Divje Babe in Slovenia. Dating from 43,000 years ago, this pierced cave-bear femur may have been manipulated to produce sounds; equally, it could simply be the result of a puncture wound.

One astonishing find near Toulouse in southern France indicates that Neanderthals did not just build for necessity but also for more cryptic reasons. Around 300 m (1,000 ft) deep in Bruniquel Cave, in an area that would have required flames to illuminate it, some ancient people arranged broken stalagmites into two circles, one of them 6 m (20 ft) across. Several stalagmites are balanced against each other and a flat surface is raised on a cylindrical rock, with more pieces placed on top – like an abstract sculpture. The rocks are heavy and arranging them in these patterns would have required hours or days of labour. Charcoal and bone remains show that burning took place for light, warmth, or possibly some unknown ceremony. By examining the spread of fresh limestone over the structure, scientists dated its construction to 176,000 years ago, when *Homo neanderthalensis* was the only hominin living around the site.

Adornments and burials suggest that Neanderthals were capable of symbolic thought, for example imagining a journey for their people after death. Could they have also had language, not just the grunts of their caricatures? Studies of Neanderthal skulls and genes have shown they may have possessed similar speech muscles to our own, and ear bones that could have given them a similar range of hearing. They weighed about 64–82 kg (140–180 lb) and grew to 1.5–1.75 m (5–5.7 ft) tall, a similar average height as *Homo sapiens*. They walked upright and were probably stronger and wider in the chest area, allowing a greater lung capacity. As for intelligence, they had slightly larger but different-shaped skulls to *Homo sapiens*, with a greater brain capacity, allowing for a larger brain.

All these findings suggest it would have been possible for Neanderthals to thrive and progress, but they must have lacked something in comparison with *Homo sapiens*. Various reasons for *Homo sapiens*'s success have been proposed by researchers. Modern humans may have been better equipped to compete for food and territory, for example by crafting better weapons and being more prepared for periods without food.

## MORE COMPETITION FOR LESS FOOD?

Neanderthals were not numerous. Scientists estimate there were fewer than 70,000 living at any one time and that they would have been widespread, living in small groups as far apart as 100 km (60 miles). As a result, they would have been susceptible to inbreeding. Neanderthals were well suited to colder climates, with wide nostrils for inhaling and warming up cold air before it reached the lungs, and stockier bodies would have coped better with chills. However, from around 55,000 years ago the climate went through relatively fast changes from hot to cold and back, which would have affected the migration patterns, and therefore the availability, of the animals Neanderthals relied upon for their meat-heavy diet.

An estimated 80 per cent of Neanderthals died before the age of 40, with some bone samples showing possible signs of bear, big cat or wolf attacks. The musculature of their arms may have made it difficult for Neanderthals to throw spears a long distance. It's more likely that they killed by thrusting spears at close quarters, putting hunters at great risk when faced with large or aggressive prey.

*Homo sapiens* and *Homo neanderthalensis* may have shared space for about 5,000 years. There is no archaeological evidence of violence between the species, although they may have competed for territory. Researchers from the universities of Cambridge and Oxford Brookes, UK, claim that Neanderthals might have been affected by infectious diseases carried out of Africa by *Homo sapiens*, such as tapeworm, tuberculosis, herpes and stomach ulcers.

Interbreeding seems to have produced some hybrids. Skeletal remains found in the Czech Republic appear to match those of modern humans but with minor Neanderthal traits, such as a bulge at the back of the skull and large wisdom teeth. It is possible that through breeding, Neanderthals were slowly assimilated into the pool of modern-day humans. Their demise seems to have been gradual, rather than a sudden, swift ending. They are thought to have been extinct by around 39,000 years ago.

Whatever the reason for their decline – and it is credible that there were multiple causes – the Neanderthals should not be regarded as a failed branch of humanity. They showed remarkable longevity and abilities comparable to those of early *Homo sapiens*. While we may not share the streets with walking *Homo neanderthalensis*, they survive today in our human DNA.

# WHERE IS THE ARK OF THE COVENANT?

The Ark of the Covenant is one of the holiest of ancient relics. Built following specifications that came directly from God, this ornamented golden casket is said to contain the stone tablets that bore the Ten Commandments, as given to Moses. It was installed in the Temple at Jerusalem but disappeared over 2,000 years ago. There are many stories of the Ark and its journey. The question of whether it still exists and where it might be resting is fascinating and, for millions, a settled point of their faith. Was the Ark of the Covenant destroyed, looted, hidden or placed in sanctuary out of view?

The Ark was first mentioned in Exodus, the second book of the Old Testament, which describes the flight of the Israelites from bondage in Egypt towards the Promised Land, led by the Hebrew prophet Moses. Having received the Ten Commandments, etched into stone tablets by the hand of God, on Mount Sinai, Moses was given specific instructions on housing them. He was to build an ark, or casket, using shittim-wood (acacia). It was to be 2.5 cubits long, 1.5 cubits wide and 1.5 cubits deep. (A cubit is around 46 cm or 18 inches, although it's not a fixed measurement.) The wood was to be lined inside and out with gold. Four golden rings were to be placed on its corners, through which golden poles could be threaded so the Ark could be carried.

The lid of the Ark, known as the 'mercy seat', was to be decorated with the figures of two cherubim, their wings raised to shield the cover. God told Moses that he would communicate with him from above these cherubim. The Ark was to be hidden behind a veil and placed in a tent of congregation called the Tabernacle when the Israelites camped during their exodus.

## TERRIFYING POWER

Once constructed and consecrated, the Ark and its contents were carried ahead of the Israelites on their journey. It displayed incredible powers; the River Jordan is supposed to have dried up as the priests carrying the Ark touched its waters, allowing the party to safely pass. It is said to have cleared the route of snakes, scorpions and thorns by firing jets of flame from its underside. On arriving at Jericho, the Ark was carried on a circuit around the city's great walls while trumpeters played, and the walls tumbled down.

The Ark is next mentioned in the Book of Samuel, where it is installed in the Temple at Shiloh (an ancient city located north of Jerusalem) before being captured in a battle against the Philistines. During the seven months that the Philistines possessed the Ark, it brought them nothing but bad fortune, including the toppling and decapitation of an idol and plagues of boils and mice. Having suffered enough of its curse, the Philistines returned the Ark to the Israelites. Next, 70 (or 50,070, sources disagree) Israelite men of Beth-shemesh were said to have been killed by God as punishment for daring to peer into the Ark. Viewing the Ark and its contents was strictly forbidden, except for a few high priests.

Under King David, the Ark was brought to Zion where it was placed in a permanent Tabernacle and occasionally brought out in times of war to support the army. David's son, King Solomon, built the First Temple of Jerusalem (completed in 957BCE) to house the Ark at the Temple Mount, where Abraham is said to have prepared to sacrifice his son. Solomon prepared a special inner sanctuary named the Holy of Holies to receive the Ark in his temple. Once installed, it is said that the Temple filled with a cloud, as 'the glory of the Lord had filled the house of the Lord'. While here, the Ark was only accessible once a year, and only by the high priest.

The Ark of the Covenant provided a direct link with God, carried the holiest of artefacts, and could protect its people and defeat their enemies. How could such an awesomely powerful and meaningful icon of faith, and symbol of the unity of a people, go missing?

## LOOTED OR HIDDEN AWAY?

The Ark is barely mentioned later on in the Bible, though one passage in Apocrypha (related ancient texts, not part of the Old Testament) states that the prophet Jeremiah, 'being warned of God', took the Ark and its portable temple, the Tabernacle, and buried them in a cave on Mount Nebo in Jordan. Jeremiah then told his followers that the hiding place should remain unknown 'until the time that God should gather His people again together, and receive them unto mercy'.

According to the Old Testament Book of Isaiah, the Ark was taken or destroyed by the Babylonians, led by Nebuchadnezzar, when they captured Jerusalem in 587BCE and destroyed Solomon's temple. If the Babylonians had claimed the Ark, it was not among the 5,400 treasures later returned by Cyrus, King of Persia and listed in the Book of Ezra. The Old Testament Book of Chronicles has it that King Josiah of Judah (639–609BCE) hid the Ark in a cave on Temple Mount before the Babylonian attack; another legend has it hidden in a cellar beneath a woodshed.

The Book of Kings records that Pharaoh Shishak (Sheshonq) took all the treasures of the temple back to Egypt when he raided Canaan in the mid-10th century BCE. Another report says the Ark was taken away from the Temple before the Romans occupied Jerusalem in 70CE and then hidden in Qumran, the site where the Dead Sea Scrolls would be discovered centuries later (page 127).

There is some visual evidence that the Romans did not obtain the Ark when they destroyed the rebuilt Second Temple in Jerusalem. In Rome's Forum, a prominent frieze on the stone Arch of Titus from 81CE shows soldiers carrying away holy treasures from the temple; a large seven-branched menorah is identifiable, but nothing resembling the Ark. Had they found it, surely Rome would have boasted about such a major trophy on this monument? Much later, the canons at the Church of Saint John Lateran (San Giovanni in Laterano) in Rome asserted that the Ark arrived there in the 12th century, was kept for 600 years and viewed by Pope Benedict XIV in 1745.

Imagined view of the Ark of the Covenant.

In 1996, the Dutch-born archaeologist Leen Ritmeyer claimed that his studies around Temple Mount had revealed the spot where he believed Solomon's Temple and Holy of Holies were located. Here, said Ritmeyer, a section of bedrock had been cut out, matching the reported dimensions of the Ark: 'a rectangular depression carved in the rocky outcropping below the dome... 2 feet 7 inches by 4 feet 4 inches'. However, it's unlikely that permission will be granted in the near future to excavate such a holy site, to follow up on Ritmeyer's convictions.

## THE ARK'S JOURNEY TO ETHIOPIA

One account of the Ark's progress and final resting place continues to be upheld by a great number of worshippers in Ethiopia. As written in the Ethiopian book of kings, *Kebra Negast*, the Ethiopian Queen of Sheba (page 23) became pregnant with Solomon's child on her visit to Jerusalem. On her return, she gave birth to a son she named Edna Lahakim, also known as Menelik. On reaching manhood, Menelik travelled to Jerusalem, where he was welcomed by King Solomon and treated as his heir. Menelik insisted on returning to Ethiopia, so Solomon ordered the first-born sons of several Israelite nobles to join him. Unbeknown to Menelik and encouraged by angels, his entourage removed the Ark from Solomon's temple and smuggled it out of Jerusalem. When the party revealed their plot on the journey to Ethiopia, Menelik danced with joy, accepting the treasure as God's will.

The earliest manuscript of the *Kebra Negast* has been tentatively dated to the 15th century. It is thought to have been written to validate claims by Ethiopian rulers that they are part of an unbroken dynasty from Solomon and Sheba. Followers of the Ethiopian Orthodox Tewahedo Church dispute the date and claim the book was copied from a 4th-century manuscript, written in the Coptic script used by Egyptian Christians and based on a much earlier account. The book contains many passages that recount stories from the Old and New Testaments, woven together with Jewish rabbinical texts and more apocryphal works. Some of the passages are contradictory or rely on the discovery of 'lost' manuscripts in support of claims of a holy lineage for the Ethiopian monarchy.

A link with Solomon and Judean nobility was claimed for generations of Ethiopian monarchs right up to the last king, Haile Selassie, who claimed to be the 225th monarch, descended from Menelik. He even had the imperial lineage written into the country's constitution.

In the Ethiopian Orthodox Christian tradition, the Ark is said to reside within the small 17th-century chapel of Maryam Seyon (Mary of Zion) in Aksum, Ethiopia. Aksum was the capital of a mighty trading empire until the end of the 7th century. The chapel is guarded by a single chaste monk who is never allowed out of the grounds. Neither he, the head of the Ethiopian Orthodox Church, nor anyone else is permitted to see what lies inside its special chamber or beneath its jewel-encrusted cloth. This is, in effect, an article of faith; for millions of Ethiopian Christians, the presence of the Ark is a fact that needs no physical proof. Once, Christian men were allowed to approach and kiss the doorpost of the chapel. Now, the faithful queue outside to receive holy water channelled through railings.

There is confusion over what exactly is kept in the chapel at Aksum. Part of the tradition in Ethiopian Orthodox churches is the use of a *tabot*, or altar tablet. This flat wood, stone or precious metal slab represents the original Ten Commandments tablets and is consecrated and guarded as a precious relic in thousands of churches – veiled and hidden from the sight of the common man. The word *tabot* is interchangeable with the Ethiopian word for a container or Ark. As such, it may be that a similar altar tablet is the treasure in the chapel of Maryam Seyon, rather than an ornamented golden casket or one of the stone tablets that Moses brought down from Mount Sinai.

There are reports of people seeing such a tablet in the chapel. In 1869 an Armenian priest, Dimotheos Sapritchian, insisted he had seen the artefact, reporting, 'The coffer was a casket of Indian work. When it was opened, they saw the Tablet of the Ten Commandments. They removed the Tablet so that they could examine it more closely. The stone was evidently pink marble of a type usually found in Egypt. It was quadrangular, 24 cm long by 22 cm wide, and only 3 cm thick. At the edges, it was decorated with engraved flowers. In the centre, there was a second quadrangular line in the form of a fine chain, and the space between the two frames contained the Ten Commandments, five on one side and five on the other, written obliquely in Turkish fashion.' Dimotheos, believing the text on the tablet to be Abyssinian (old Ethiopian) rather than Hebrew, dismissed the tablet as a forgery.

Rather than an ornate golden Ark that would be familiar to fans of the Indiana Jones film *Raiders of the Lost Ark*, it seems the chapel may house one of the tablets that the Ark was meant to contain. After 3,000 years and many journeys across the Holy Land, a gold-coated wooden casket would not have survived well without divine assistance. The timbers would surely have rotted, but the stones inside may have survived. Even so, there is much doubt that the relic protected in a small chapel in Aksum is what it purports to be.

Keeping it hidden may be the best option, in order for it to retain its mystique.

# HOW DID ROME'S NINTH LEGION DISAPPEAR?

The successful expansion of the Roman Empire was due to the strength and discipline of its armed troops. Their conquests are recorded in many histories, tributes, journals and letters. There are numerous legions who won great victories in battle and some that fell and were even annihilated by local forces. The Ninth Legion, however, is infamous as the Roman legion that disappeared entirely from the record books. Where did thousands of elite professional soldiers go, and why is there no account of the Ninth Legion's final mission?

Rome's army was divided into 30 or so large units called legions; a typical legion consisted of about 4,200 infantry and 300 cavalry. All professional soldiers and Roman citizens, legionaries signed up for as long as 25 years and were promised a good pension at the end of their service. Each *legio* (legion) was under the command of a Roman senator called a *legatus legionis* (legate) and, below the legate, six *tribuni militum* or military tribunes. Next in rank, officer-class centurions gave orders to 80 men below them. Six *centuria* of 80 men each formed a cohort, and 10 cohorts a legion.

Legionaries were trained to fight on the battlefield, attack fortresses and even serve aboard ships. They were also employed during peacetime to construct roads, bridges, aqueducts, garrisons and walls, like the famed Hadrian's Wall, which bordered England and Scotland. A Roman soldier might spend years away from home and family, stationed on the border of the empire in northern England or the Persian Gulf.

## NUMBERED AND PROUDLY NAMED

Roman legions were both numbered and given names. Some of the numbers lasted for centuries, although their titles and personnel would change. Others came to an end in battle, or were disbanded for disobedience, and their legion numbers discarded. Three entire legions under the governor Publius Quinctilius Varus – the 17th, 18th and 19th (XVII, XVIII and XIX) – were destroyed in a major conflict in the Teutoberg Forest in modern-day Germany in 9CE. Some of the sites where Roman soldiers fell were located in 1987, in fields north of Osnabrück. This crushing defeat struck the Emperor Augustus hard and these legion numbers were never re-used.

The legions I *Germanica* ('Victor over the Germans'), IV *Macedonia* ('Victor over the Macedonians'), V *Alaudae* ('The Larks'), XV *Primigenia* ('First Born') and XVI *Gallica* ('Victor over the Gauls') were also defeated during a period of civil war in 69CE known as 'The Year of the Four Emperors'. As a result, I, V and XV were disbanded, while IV and XVI were replaced by new legions, IV *Flavia Felix* ('The Lucky Flavian') and XVI *Flavia Firma* ('The Steadfast Flavian').

Of the legions that disappeared without an epitaph, XXI *Rapax* ('Grasping') met its fate towards the end of the 1st century CE. It may have fallen in conflict against the Dacians (from modern-day Romania) around 90CE. Legion XXII (*Deiotariana* or 'Deiotarus's 22nd') disappeared in Egypt after 119CE, perhaps in a struggle against the Judeans. But the legion whose disappearance seems most mysterious is that of the Ninth Legion, or *Legio IX Hispana* (Spain). The British antiquarian John Horsley recorded details of every Roman legion's movements within Britain in his 1732 book *Britannia Romana (The Roman Antiquities of Britain)*, but he could not provide a date when the Ninth Legion left.

## THE NINTH AND CAESAR

The earliest record of the Ninth Legion has it taking part in a siege in Asculum, north-east of Rome, during the Social War of 90BCE. The Ninth later campaigned across Gaul from 58BCE under the command of Julius Caesar, and fought at Dyrrhachium (Albania) and Pharsalus (Greece) in 48BCE, and across Africa in 46BCE. After his final victory, Caesar disbanded the Ninth Legion and allowed veterans to settle in Picenum, Italy.

After Caesar's assassination in 44BCE, his ally Ventidius Bassus attempted to reassemble three of Caesar's legions, including the Ninth. They were recalled by Caesar's successor Octavian to put down a rebellion led by Sextus Pompeius (son of Caesar's defeated rival, Pompey the Great) in Sicily. After losing this battle, they were moved to Macedonia and later fought at the decisive naval battle at Actium against Mark Antony in 31BCE.

When Octavian was declared sole ruler of Rome, the Ninth Legion was sent on a tour of duty in Spain, where they probably gained the name *Hispana*. By 13BCE, the legion could be found in the Balkans (in present-day Croatia), before being sent as part of an invasion force to Britannia (Britain) much later, in 43CE. The Ninth settled in Britannia as part of a garrison.

The records, including Roman graves, show the soldiers were based in Linden Colonia (now Lincoln) in the year 60CE, where they defeated a revolt led by Venutius, King of the British Brigantes people. They were less successful during the rebellion of Boudicca, Queen of the Iceni people of modern-day Norfolk, a year later. Most of the Ninth's infantry were wiped out in an attempt to relieve the besieged city of Camulodunum (Colchester). After reinforcements arrived from the provinces of Germania, the Ninth were led to victory under the governor Cerialis, defeating the Brigantes once more.

## TRACES IN NORTHERN ENGLAND

One of the last certain records of the Ninth Legion saw them in Eboracum (York), building a gateway for a new stone fortress around 107–108CE. In 1854, workmen digging a drain in York found part of a large commemorative tablet from the period that scholars have been able to complete and translate as 'The Emperor Caesar Nerva Trajan Augustus, son of the deified Nerva, Conqueror of Germany, Conqueror of Dacia, Chief Priest, in his twelfth year of tribunician power [108CE], acclaimed imperator six times... through the agency of the Ninth Hispana Legion'.

Early assumptions were that the legion was defeated in struggles in northern Britain, around 115–17CE. According to the 19th-century German historian Theodor Mommsen, 'under Hadrian there was a terrible catastrophe here, apparently an attack on the fortress of Eboracum and the annihilation of the legion stationed there, the very same Ninth that had fought so unluckily in the Boudican revolt'.

Emperor Hadrian is on record requesting the assistance of the Sixth Legion (VI *Victrix* or 'Victorious') in 122CE, when he ordered the building of his great wall on the northern border because 'the Britons could not be kept under Roman control'. Three legions, including the Sixth, worked on the wall and left their mark. The Ninth, however, is notable for its absence. The Sixth Legion may have arrived as a replacement for the Ninth and did take over the Ninth's barracks in York.

As noted by the German historian and archaeologist Emil Ritterling in 1925, 'The transfer of VI Victrix to Britain had been caused by a dangerous uprising... The revolt was significant in that, not only was an entire legion transferred to the island for the duration, but vexillations of 1,000 men each were drawn from the two Upper German legions and the Spanish legion.'

The classic portrayal is of the Ninth marching out to subdue troublesome Caledonian (Scottish) raiders, and mysteriously

Remains of a Roman fort along Hadrian's Wall.

vanishing in the mist and into history on the border with Scotland. 'Sometime about the year AD117, the Ninth Legion, which was stationed at Eburacum where York now stands, marched north to deal with a rising among the Caledonian tribes, and was never heard of again.... no one knows what happened to the Ninth Legion after it marched into the northern mists.' These words are from Rosemary Sutcliff's 1954 children's novel, *The Eagle of the Ninth*. Sutcliff's story was inspired by the discovery of a small bronze eagle in Silchester, Hampshire, in southern England.

Her story involved a centurion, Marcus Flavius Aquila, heading into Scotland to discover the fate of his father, chief centurion of the Ninth Legion, and to retrieve the legion's golden *aquila* (eagle) emblem carried with pride by the legion's *aquilifer*, or standard bearer. The loss of a legion's eagle standard was considered a major dishonour. It represented not only the legion but the might of Rome itself. The statuette that inspired the novel more likely belonged to a cult following the god Jupiter rather than the Ninth Legion, but this did not prevent a great deal of mythologizing around the ancient find. Indeed, the novel was later adapted into both a TV series and a film, *The Eagle*, in 2011.

## DID THE LOST LEGION LEAVE BRITANNIA?

It may be that the Ninth did not fall in Britain at all. The British historian and archaeologist Professor Sheppard Frere suggested that the legion was withdrawn from Britain between 108 and 120CE. Potential evidence for this are traces of the legion at Noviomagus Batavorum (Nijmegen) in the Netherlands, perhaps later than 115–17CE. An inscribed pendant from a horse harness was found close to Nijmegen, stamped 'LEG IX HISP'. Evidence at the site of a legionary fortress on the lower River Rhine includes several roofing tiles stamped as the property of the Ninth. An altar to Apollo found near Aachen in Germany was erected under orders of Lucius Licinius Macer, the commander of the Ninth Legion. Whether or not this was proof that the entire Ninth Legion or a detachment was sent back to mainland Europe is debated. None of these findings can be accurately dated.

From here, the legion may have marched on to Judea and fought during the Second Jewish Revolt, known as the Bar-Kokhba Revolt, of 132–35CE. Alternatively, they could have joined Marcus Aurelius in the war against Parthia from 161 to 166CE. In 161CE Governor Marcus Sedatius Severianus committed suicide when he realized the legion he was commanding faced certain doom against the Parthians in Armenia. Indeed, the unspecified Roman legion were massacred. There were two legions recorded as being based nearby, in Cappadocia (in modern-day Türkiye). These were the XII *Fulminata* and XV *Apollonaris*, both of which survived to fight many decades later. Could this mean, therefore, that the unnamed legion that was annihilated in Armenia was the Ninth?

What is not in doubt is that the Ninth Legion had ended its service by around 197CE during the reign of Emperor Septimius Severus (193–211CE), because it is not listed as one of the 33 extant legions at that time. The loss of the Ninth Legion in the north of Britain seems the most likely solution to this mystery – its eagle emblem irretrievable or deliberately hidden to avoid disgrace. Some historians argue that the lost legion's legacy is Hadrian's Wall itself, built as a permanent border. One day, perhaps, archaeologists will unearth something beyond the wall in ancient Caledonia that marks a battlefield, and the soldiers of the Ninth can be memorialized. Until then, the search for the lost legion continues.

# WHAT BECAME OF THE HOLY GRAIL?

The Holy Grail is said to be the cup that Jesus drank from at the Last Supper and the chalice that collected his blood at the crucifixion. While understood to be a Christian relic, the tale of the Grail and its quest is inextricably tied to Arthurian legends and may have been inspired by earlier Celtic myths. Was the Grail a pagan artefact or a holy relic brought to Europe by saints or knights? And what became of this most sought-after treasure?

While the adventures of King Arthur (page 209) and his retinue of knights are firmly set in ancient Britain, it is in France that their stories were given flesh, particularly in the chivalric romances of Chrétien de Troyes. Chrétien wrote his Arthurian poems around 1170–90, often giving Arthur only a minor role. Of the five he worked on, the final tale, *Perceval* or *The Story of the Grail*, was unfinished at the time of Chrétien's death, although it became one of the most influential by introducing the concept of the quest for the Holy Grail.

In Chrétien's tale, Perceval is an innocent boy brought up in a forest who is introduced to Arthur's court and taken under the wing of an older knight named Governal. Governal trains Perceval in the ways of chivalry and advises him never to speak out of turn or ask foolish questions out of curiosity. This advice does not prove advantageous for Perceval.

On one adventure, Perceval is directed to a remote castle. Upon entering it he witnesses a procession, including a servant carrying a white lance that drips blood from its point and two boys carrying candleholders. Finally, the legend says, 'A girl entered with them, holding a grail-dish in both her hands – a beautiful girl, elegant, extremely well dressed. And as she walked into the hall, holding this grail, it glowed with so great a light that the candles suddenly seemed to grow dim, like the moon and stars when the sun appears in the sky.' The word 'grail' is translated from the old French word *graal*, meaning cup or chalice, although it is portrayed more as a wide dish in Chrétien's poem. This grail is made of the purest gold and studded with many jewels. It is used to provide food for a wounded man known as the Fisher King who is understood to be the last in a line of British kings charged with guarding this holy relic.

Perceval's story then strays and the knight Gawain enters in search of the very same Grail. Chrétien's poem ends mid-sentence, but his mystery of the Grail was so compelling that over the next 50 years other writers took up the challenge of completing the work, altering or elaborating his plot.

## A CHRISTIAN DIMENSION IS ADDED

Robert de Boron, a French writer from the late 12th and early 13th century, is thought to have been working on a Grail trilogy involving Perceval, Merlin and Joseph of Arimathea, though only works on the latter two subjects survive in some form, and in translation. De Boron was the first to identify the Grail as the cup used by Jesus at the Last Supper. The legend now had a Christian dimension. In de Boron's *Joseph d'Arimathie*, Joseph of Arimathea was a disciple of Jesus who used the same cup to catch Christ's blood at the crucifixion. Joseph does appear in all four gospels in the New Testament. He takes responsibility for burying Christ after the crucifixion, gathers a linen shroud (see page 139) and places the body in a sealed cave, or possibly his own tomb.

The Gospel of Matthew mentions Jesus drinking from a cup during the Last Supper: 'And He took a cup and when He had given thanks He gave it to them saying "Drink this, all of you; for this is My blood of the covenant, which is poured out for many for the forgiveness of sins. I tell you, I shall not drink again of the fruit of the vine until I drink it new with you in My Father's kingdom."' However, there is no mention of the cup being retained or of Joseph of Arimathea using such a vessel to collect Christ's blood. The mythology of the Grail only comes alive following the European tales of King Arthur's knights.

Of particular note in expanding the Arthurian legend of the Grail are early 13th-century continuations by Waucheir de Denain and Manessier, who had Perceval claim the throne of the Fisher King, along with his Grail and Lance before carrying them to Heaven upon his death.

The most complete Grail story also appeared in the early 13th century in five separate stories called the Vulgate Cycle, or Lancelot-Grail Cycle. Attributed to unnamed French monks or clerics from the Cistercian order, the saga covers the life of King Arthur but is also notable for its Grail mythology. The *Vulgate Estoire del Saint Graal* (*Story of the Holy Grail*) has Joseph of Arimathea and his son, Josephus, carrying the Grail from the Holy Land to Britain, where they begin converting the pagan populace and founding Christian churches. On their death, their relics, including the Grail, are placed in a castle called Corbenic. A line of 'Grail kings', who guard the holy chalice, is listed, the Arthurian knights Lancelot and Gawain among them, leading up to Pelleam,

*The Achievement of the Grail* (1891–4), tapestry based on designs by Edward Burne-Jones, with Galahad kneeling before the Holy Grail.

who sports a mysterious, unhealing wound, matching that of the aforementioned Fisher King.

## THE QUEST ENDS

The *Vulgate Queste del Saint Graal* (*Quest for the Holy Grail*) has Perceval making his entrance into the court of King Arthur as a teenager. He is directed to sit on the 'Siege Perilous': the chair beside Arthur that is reserved for the one who will find the Grail. And as they sit for supper, they feel the light of the Holy Spirit upon them and 'there entered the Holy Grail covered with a white cloth; but no one was able to see who was carrying it. It entered by the great door of the hall, and as soon as it had come in, the hall was filled with odours as sweet as if all the spices of the earth were diffused there. And it passed down the middle of the hall and all around the high seats; and as it passed before the tables, they were straightway filled at each place with such viands as the occupant desired. When all were served, the Holy Grail departed at once so that they knew not what had become of it nor did they see which way it went.'

The knights determine to seek out this Grail. Gawain is the first to head out but is forewarned by a hermit that he is too concerned with worldly matters and women to be spiritual enough to succeed in his mission. Lancelot is similarly unable to claim the Grail, due to the taint of his adulterous affair with King Arthur's beloved wife Guinevere. Galahad, however, is the most devout of all the knights and effectively takes on the role that Chrétien de Troyes gave to Perceval. The illegitimate son of Lancelot and Elaine, daughter of the Fisher King, he travels for over five years until he reaches Corbenic Castle. When Galahad is shown the Grail, he peers into it and cries, 'Here I behold the motive of courage and the inspiration of prowess; here I see the marvel of marvels!' Overcome, Galahad then prostrates himself and ascends to Heaven, along with the Grail. The quest for the Grail was told again in the 15th century, in *Le Morte D'Arthur*, Sir Thomas Malory's faster-paced version of the legend of King Arthur.

Does the story of the Grail predate the Knights of the Round Table? Chrétien de Troyes and later writers may have been inspired by earlier folkloric tales. Several Celtic and Welsh myths feature cauldrons with restorative powers. The Welsh *Mabinogion* collects tales possibly from the 11th and 12th centuries, that feature a giant king called Brân the Blessed, who is given a cauldron that can bring the dead to life. Even earlier is the classical myth of the horn of plenty, or cornucopia: a horn-shaped vessel that provided unlimited nourishment.

## THE GRAIL ON DISPLAY

And what of the chalice itself? Was there a physical Grail that was preserved from the time of Jesus that was transported from the Holy Land? Long before the tales of Arthur were written, a 6th-century pilgrim, sometimes named Antonius of Piacenza, reported seeing 'the cup of onyx, which our Lord blessed at the last supper' among relics displayed in a sanctuary at the Basilica of Constantine in Golgotha, near Jerusalem. The 7th-century Frankish pilgrim Arculf also claimed, in journals of his travels, that Jesus's cup was displayed near Jerusalem. In the late 12th century, the same cup was said to be in the imperial chapel in Byzantium (modern-day Istanbul, Türkiye) before being carried away to Troyes, France, when the city was looted by the crusaders in 1204.

Today, there are two items on public display that make claims of being or resembling the Holy Grail. The Sacro Catino (Sacred Basin) at Genoa Cathedral is a green glass dish rumoured to have been brought to Italy by Crusaders in the 12th century. Its association with the Last Supper only came about following interest in the Arthurian romances, though, and the dish is now thought to be of Islamic origin.

The Holy Chalice of Valencia in the Cathedral of Valencia, Spain, is an agate dish thought to be much older, from ancient Greek or Roman times, and one that undertook a convoluted journey. According to the Cathedral, the chalice was brought to Rome by Saint Peter and used by successive popes in Eucharistic celebrations. In the year 258CE Pope Sixtus II ordered it to be smuggled out of Rome to keep it from Emperor Valerian, who was persecuting Christians at the time. The pope's deacon, St Lawrence, carried the cup to Huesca, Spain, where his parents lived, and hid it in the monastery of San Juan de la Peña where it was listed in an inventory in 1134. In 1399 it was donated to King Martin I of Aragón after which it was passed to the Cathedral of

Valencia. The cup was considered a holy relic and continued to be used by popes to celebrate Mass. In 1982 Pope John Paul II described it as 'a witness to Christ's passage on Earth'.

The claims of these two chalices being holy relics are flimsy, and unlikely to stop modern-day 'knights' from seeking an undisputed Grail. While it seems to have been an invention of medieval poets, the story of a cup touched by the Son of God being kept safe by disciples and chevaliers for thousands of years retains a magic that will surely endure.

# DID THE VIKINGS BEAT COLUMBUS TO THE AMERICAS?

Scandinavian raiders, or Vikings, were notorious for their attacks on the coasts of Europe from the 8th century. They raided, traded and ultimately settled abroad, reaching lands far beyond their homes in present-day Denmark, Iceland, Norway and Sweden. But one of the great mysteries around their adventures is whether they reached the coast of North America hundreds of years before Christopher Columbus crossed the Atlantic. It's also possible that pre-Columbian murals show Scandinavians captured by the Maya, so could they have also pushed much further south in the Americas?

There is no doubt that Norsemen were hugely confident sailors. They crossed the Caspian Sea for Baghdad, and navigated into eastern Europe along the Dnieper and Volga rivers to attack Constantinople and, as the 'Rus', gave their name to Russia. They also sailed west to settle on Iceland and Greenland.

Norse voyages to distant lands are described in their lengthy sagas, which were transcribed 300 years or so after the events, and therefore may be mythologized to some extent. According to the *Saga of Erik the Red*, at some time in the late 10th century the Norwegian Erik Thorvaldsson was exiled as punishment for killing his neighbours, following a dispute over the death of his thralls (slaves). He went from Norway to Iceland, but after further confrontations and killings he was ordered to leave Iceland too.

Erik sailed west in the direction of land glimpsed by another Norwegian almost a century before. After arriving there he called it Greenland, supposedly 'because men will desire much the more to go there if the land has a good name'. (At that time, during the Medieval Warm Period, the southern coasts of Greenland were not as snow-covered and frozen as today.) Erik spent three years exploring before returning to Iceland and persuading a large number of his countrymen to return with him. Of 25 ships that set off, 14 arrived and established two colonies on the south-west coast of Greenland.

## LEIF ERIKSON'S ACCIDENTAL DISCOVERY

The same saga tells of Erik's son, Leif, whose own voyage from Norway to Greenland around the year 1000 was blown off course by changing winds. Leif Erikson and his crew arrived on the shores of a foreign land (now understood as the North American

L'Anse aux Meadows Viking longhouse, Newfoundland and Labrador, Canada.

continent). There, they found wild grapes, wheat and maple trees growing. They gathered stocks of these and sailed back to Greenland to report on their discovery. An alternative version in the *Saga of the Greenlanders* has Leif following a sighting by an earlier merchant, Bjarni Herjóldsson, and leading a crew of 35 men to a coast 'level and wooded, with broad white beaches'. He named this place Helluland or 'Slab Land'; it may be today's Baffin Island.

He then reached a more inviting forested coast that he named, in an equally unimaginative fashion, Markland ('Forest Land'), which is thought to be the region of Labrador in north-eastern Canada. Further south the voyagers found 'wine-berries' growing, so Leif named the area Vinland ('Wineland'). This may be the area around the Gulf of St Lawrence in eastern Canada.

The explorers built a small settlement named Leifsbudir ('Leif's camp') on this coast to last them over winter, before some returned to Greenland.

Leif's brother Thorvald stayed at the same camp for another year, but was killed in a local conflict. In 1025, Thorfinn Karlsefni led a group of 65 colonizers to Vinland, where they stayed for three years. Thorfinn's wife Gudrid gave birth to a son, Snorri, on Vinland, the first European to be born in the New World. These settlers were also attacked by locals they called *skrælings* ('wretches') and eventually they chose to return home. According to the *Saga of Erik the Red*, 'though the land might be choice and good, there would be always war and terror overhanging them, from those who dwelt there before them. They made ready, therefore, to move away, with intent to go to their own land.' Despite the occasional violence between the Norse and indigenous people, voyages between Greenland and North America continued for a few hundred years, with the Scandinavians harvesting timber and trading with locals for furs and skins.

The sagas' accounts of Scandinavian sailors settling in North America were treated with scepticism for centuries, although these adventures were apparently not forgotten. Around 1069, the German churchman Adam of Bremen claimed that the King of Denmark himself had told him of a land to the west, writing, 'He spoke of an island in that ocean discovered by many, which is called Wineland, for the reason that vines grow wild there, which yield the best of wine. Moreover, that grain unsown grows there abundantly is not a fabulous fancy, but from the accounts of the Danes we know to be a fact. Beyond this island, it is said. there is no habitable land in that ocean, but all those regions which are beyond are filled with insupportable ice and boundless gloom.'

## WRITTEN AND SYMBOLIC EVIDENCE

Aside from Icelandic and other Norse sagas, what evidence exists for the Vikings reaching the Americas centuries before Columbus's landmark voyage in 1492? *The Flatey Book*, written by the priests John Thordsson and Magnus Thorhallsson in 1387, contains passages describing the colonies in Vinland. The discovery of North America by Scandinavians was also reported in Latin history books written by the Icelander Arngrim Jonsson in the early 17th century, and in the work of the Icelandic historian Thormod Torfæus a century later. Even so, the possibility that Vikings had reached North America by the 11th century was left as a footnote in histories of Columbus's maritime ventures.

As for physical evidence to back up the written reports, markings carved into Dighton Rock, a boulder found in Massachusetts, were thought to include Viking runes translated as 'Thorfinn and his 151 companions took possession of this land.' The deciphered symbols sit among many other marks and petroglyphs (images cut into rock). They are now thought to be the work of the indigenous Algonquin Indian people.

The Skálholt Map, designed by an Icelandic teacher named Sigurdur Stefansson around 1590, depicted the lands named by Leif Erikson across the Atlantic. Known only from a copy, it appears to be an interpretation from the sagas, rather than based on accurate charts. A Vinland Map, supposedly from around 1440, was purchased by Yale University in 1965 but is now considered to be a fake.

It seemed that the sagas were to remain the only 'proof' that Scandinavians reached North America over a thousand years ago. Then, archaeological work in the 1960s by the Norwegians Anne Stine and Helge Ingstad found evidence of Norse settlements from the period 990–1050, with a specific date of 1021 being pinpointed by studies of tree-ring samples. On the northern tip of the island of Newfoundland (now part of the Canadian province of Newfoundland and Labrador), they found a site known as L'Anse aux Meadows, where there were ruins of several turf-built structures with timber roofs. The site included the remains of houses which could have provided accommodation for up to 90 people, a smithy and boathouse. Small finds included many iron rivets, a clothes pin, a spindle and a lamp, all Norwegian in design. L'Anse aux Meadows appears to have been used as a base camp for ship repairs before settlers explored further south. More recent excavations support accounts in the sagas that Norsemen also stopped on Baffin Island and Labrador.

## BLOND STRANGERS IN MEXICO?

Since then, no further physical evidence of Norse expeditions away from the north-east Canadian coast has been found. Nevertheless, there have been discoveries that could suggest Vikings managed to travel further south into the continent. One of the most intriguing came about from interpretations of murals in the Temple of the Warriors at Chichen Itza in Mexico. The murals show dark-skinned Maya warriors leading paler prisoners; the captured figures are decorated with horizontal stripes. Another scene shows an apparently naked, pale-skinned figure with long blond hair being held down for a sacrifice. Could these be Norsemen?

The possibility of Scandinavians reaching Mexico also stems from the *Saga of the Ere-Dwellers*, which tells of two Icelanders, Björn Breiðvíkingakappi (*c.*965) and Gudleif Gudlaugson (*c.*1025). Faced with fighting a duel, in 998 Björn left on a ship sailing westward that disappeared. Thirty years later, Gudleif and his crew set off on a merchant voyage west to Dublin but were blown off course and arrived on an unfamiliar shore. They were taken prisoner by the indigenous people and brought before their leader for slavery or execution. To their surprise, the leader was an aged, white-skinned man with a red beard who spoke in Norse and promised to set them free but did not reveal his identity. As Gudleif prepared to leave, the leader handed him a gold ring and sword to deliver to people he once knew in Iceland, but forbade further voyages to seek him out, 'for this land lacks all peace, unless to such as it may befall to come aland in such lucky wise as ye have done'. Over a year later, Gudleif returned to Iceland and delivered the ring and sword, discovering that the man that saved them was Björn Breiðvíkingakappi.

Some have tried to link this story to the Mesoamerican murals and connect the Norseman with Mayan beliefs of a white-skinned deity: an incarnation of Quetzalcoatl, their feathered serpent god. Viking ships often had a dragon head carved on to the prow, so could this have been mistaken for a serpent? Did the arrival of Björn match up with a 520-year cycle of Quetzalcoatl returning, that also delivered the conquistador Hernan Cortes in 1518? As the archaeological surveys of north-east Canada have shown, the sagas do have some basis in fact. However, it is far harder to prove that a Scandinavian presiding over a foreign tribe in Mexico was a reality.

As fascinating as these connections may be, they are probably just coincidences. There is nothing in the saga that pinpoints where Gudleif Gudlaugson was captured. The Yucatan is a long distance south from Labrador, and sailors would encounter many other American and Caribbean lands before reaching Mexico. Also, the pale figures in the murals cannot definitely be identified as European.

While archaeological evidence supports the assertion that Scandinavians reached North America centuries before Columbus, and they occupied land on and off for years, the possibility of them reaching Mesoamerica around the same time is extremely unlikely. Neither did the Scandinavian settlers make much impact on the continent. There is no record of them in the histories of the indigenous Americans. They came, they farmed, they left and their turf buildings sank into the landscape. Then, about 400 years later, the 'New World' would be rediscovered and everything would change.

# WHERE IS CLEOPATRA'S TOMB?

Cleopatra is the most captivating character from the long history of ancient Egypt: the last of its queens, a ruthless beauty, a shrewd negotiator in numerous languages, leader of armies and seducer of statesmen. She is memorialized in art, literature, theatre and film, but her final destination remains unknown. Where is the tomb of Cleopatra and her Roman lover, Mark Antony?

Cleopatra VII Philopator was born in Alexandria, Egypt in 69BCE, the daughter of Ptolemy XII, King of Egypt (r.80–51BCE). Egypt at that time was in some decline, faced with the increasing might of Rome, which had already taken Egypt-ruled Cyrenaica (eastern Libya) and had its sights on Egypt itself. Ptolemy attempted to placate this predatory power by raising taxes and providing the Roman general and consul Pompey with 8,000 Egyptian cavalrymen to support Roman expansion into Palestine. In 59BCE Ptolemy agreed to pay the equivalent of half of Egypt's annual revenue in exchange for Rome officially recognizing him as King of Egypt. It made little difference: a year later, Rome ousted Ptolemy's brother from Cyprus and added the island to its possessions.

Ptolemy's attempts to appease the Romans almost bankrupted his country. He was forced out by the angry citizenship of Alexandria and his throne was passed on to his eldest daughter, Berenike. Ptolemy went to Rome, and attempted to rule Egypt from exile for two years. He took out a loan from a Roman banker named Rabirius that was equivalent to Egypt's entire annual income to finance an expedition to reclaim power. Led by Gabinius, the Roman governor of Syria, the army took control of Alexandria in 57BCE. Ptolemy ordered the death of his daughter Berenike and made Rabirius his finance minister.

It's likely that Cleopatra accompanied Ptolemy during his exile and returned to power with him. He proclaimed her his co-regent in 52BCE, and when he died a year later Cleopatra became Queen of Egypt aged 17. As a woman, Cleopatra was expected to share the throne with her eldest brother, ten-year-old Ptolemy XIII. Her early years in power were blighted by crop failures and resulting food shortages. The populace turned against her, as did her brother, and the siblings formed rival factions.

## CLEOPATRA, CAESAR AND MARK ANTONY

In 49BCE, Pompey's son Gnaeus Pompeius arrived in Alexandria, asking for military aid in the civil war between his father and the

Roman general Julius Caesar. Cleopatra and Ptolemy provided 60 ships and 500 troops in partial payment of their country's debt to Rome. Shortly after, Ptolemy's advisers acted to depose Cleopatra and she was forced to leave Egypt, heading to Roman-controlled Syria, where she raised an army and plotted her return. She would soon be presented with an opportunity.

Pompey was roundly defeated by Caesar's forces and sought refuge in Egypt. Not wishing Egypt to become a base for Roman civil war, and hoping to curry favour with the victor, Ptolemy had Pompey killed on arrival. His head was embalmed and delivered to Caesar. However, Caesar was not entirely happy to receive this 'gift'. He arrived in Alexandria, demanding reconciliation between Ptolemy and Cleopatra. According to the historian Plutarch, Cleopatra had herself smuggled into the royal palace hidden in a wool sack and met Caesar alone. Cleopatra was now 21 years old and Caesar 31 years her elder. She charmed him with her wit and beauty.

Ptolemy was furious about this meeting and incited a city riot. Caesar attempted to calm things down by proclaiming Ptolemy and Cleopatra as joint heirs, but it was to no avail. Soon, Cleopatra and Caesar found themselves under siege in the palace. Roman reinforcements had to be called in to save the couple from Ptolemy's forces. Ptolemy drowned in the Nile while attempting to escape. Cleopatra was queen again, now sharing power with her 12-year-old brother Ptolemy XIV, and Rome had an occupying army in Egypt.

While Caesar returned to campaigning, Cleopatra gave birth to his son, whom she named Ptolemy Caesar, or Caesarion ('Little Caesar'). She then spent two years with Caesar, staying on his estate near the Tiber while Ptolemy XIV took charge in Egypt. Caesar dedicated a statue to his Egyptian lover in the Roman shrine of Venus Genetrix, and began work on a Senate bill to allow him to take Cleopatra as a second wife. The marriage would never be ratified; Caesar was assassinated on 15 March 44BCE.

Cleopatra hoped Caesarion would be recognized as Caesar's heir, but instead Caesar's great-nephew Octavian was named. The Eternal City was no longer safe for Cleopatra so she returned to Alexandria. A month later her brother was dead, poisoned on Cleopatra's orders, making Cleopatra the sole ruler.

In the wake of Caesar's death, different parties sought control. Cleopatra formed an alliance with Caesar's ally, the general Mark Antony. She arrived to meet him in Tarsus in Anatolia (in modern-day Türkiye) by a river, and arranged extravagant banquets for Antony and his troops. Within a year, the pair were together in Alexandria, the parents of twins: Alexander Helios ('sun') and Cleopatra Selene ('moon'). Almost immediately, Antony returned to Rome, where he forged an alliance with Octavian by marrying his sister, Octavia.

Over the next three years, Egypt's harvest improved, but it remained burdened by its great debts to Rome. Antony returned in 37BCE, offering territories around the Mediterranean in exchange for Egypt's support in a campaign again the Parthians, Rome's foe to the east. It was, initially, a military disaster for Antony but he continued in its pursuit. His relationship with Cleopatra was rekindled and she bore him a second son, Ptolemy Philadelphus. After a limited victory over Armenia, Antony and Cleopatra celebrated and Antony proclaimed their sons to be the future rulers of the eastern Roman Empire.

While Antony coveted the east, Octavian sought sole rule of the whole Roman Empire. Antony cut off ties with Octavia and war

Cleopatra presenting her son Ptolemy Caesar, 'Caesarian', to the gods of Egypt, relief *c.*46BCE.

broke out. The endgame was in sight after the Battle of Actium in 31BCE, when Antony and Cleopatra's navy was routed. The pair fled with just 60 ships remaining from their fleet of 230. Cleopatra offered to abdicate if Octavian would allow her children to rule in her place, but he never responded to her plea. On 1 August 31BCE, Octavian's armies reached Alexandria, Antony was defeated and Cleopatra sought sanctuary in her mausoleum.

Misinformed that Cleopatra was dead, Antony tried to kill himself and was carried to Cleopatra's side to perish. The queen was captured and imprisoned in the royal palace. Not wanting to be paraded in chains through Rome as a war trophy, Cleopatra took her own life – perhaps with snake poison or a poisoned comb. Days later, on Octavian's orders, Caesarion was assassinated. The children of Antony and Cleopatra were removed for Rome to be raised as Roman citizens. Egypt was now fully in the hands of Rome.

There would be no humiliation for Cleopatra in Rome. Instead, the Roman historians Suetonius and Plutarch claimed that Octavian, the future Augustus and Rome's first emperor, gave permission for her to be buried alongside Antony in regal fashion. But, where exactly were they entombed?

## SEEKING THE QUEEN'S TOMB

In the 19th century, Napoleon Bonaparte led unsuccessful efforts to find Cleopatra's tomb in Egypt. The majority of Egyptologists and archaeologists believe the tomb to be in or close to Alexandria. The 1st-century CE Greek writer Plutarch thought it was near the Temple of Isis at Philae, located close to Aswan in southern Egypt. This is plausible, because Cleopatra deliberately sought to identify herself with Isis. Statues were built in her lifetime, blurring the image of the queen with this important ancient Egyptian mother goddess. However, the Greek historian Strabo, who died around 21CE, claimed the tomb was on the island of Antirhodos in the eastern harbour of Alexandria.

Any trace of Antirhodos is now underwater, possibly due to a major earthquake and tsunami in 365CE. The French archaeologist Franck Goddio spent 25 years surveying the bay around Alexandria and found many traces from the Ptolemaic period, including the remains of a palace and a temple dedicated to Isis. Goddio believes the tomb to be located somewhere between these buildings.

Should the tomb be found, it may not contain two bodies. According to Plutarch, Mark Anthony was cremated. In his biographies, *The Parallel Lives*, Plutarch wrote, 'After Cleopatra had heard this, in the first place, she begged Octavian that she might be permitted to pour libations for Antony; and when the request was granted, she had herself carried to the tomb, and embracing the urn which held his ashes…'. Plutarch believed a tomb was already prepared before the death of Cleopatra, and that it was a structure above ground. His words, however, were written more than 100 years after these events.

Alexandria was founded by Alexander the Great in 331BCE and it is here that he is said to have been eventually reburied long after his death, in a great central necropolis known as the Soma, where the Ptolemaic dynasty was traditionally interred too. As part of the same dynasty, Cleopatra could conceivably have been laid to rest here. Sadly, there is no longer any trace of the Soma, the palaces of the Ptolemies, the Great Library of Alexandria and the Pharos lighthouse. Much of the ancient city of Alexandria was destroyed following the same cataclysm that sunk Antirhodos in 365CE.

From 2008, excavations led by Dominican archaeologist Kathleen Martínez on land at Taposiris Magna, 40 km (25 miles) west of Alexandria, have uncovered 27 tombs of Egyptian nobles, plus coins bearing Cleopatra's image. In November 2022, Martínez's team found a 1,305-m (4,281-ft) tunnel dug 13 m (43 ft) below the ground, which they hoped might lead to the elusive tomb; this is now thought to be an aqueduct.

The Egyptologist Zahi Hawass, former Egyptian Minister for Antiquities, disputes the idea that Cleopatra would be buried under a temple, but said in 2009, 'If we discover the tomb of Cleopatra and Mark Antony, it will be the most important discovery of the 21st century.'

Certainly, such a find would provide many answers in regard to Cleopatra and Mark Antony's final moments. Any artefacts contained within would tell us more about this enigmatic female pharaoh's life, culture and religion. The tomb is unlikely to include treasures on a scale of those found in Tutankhamun's burial complex. Nonetheless, it would be a marvellous and celebrated discovery, such is the attraction of the last queen of ancient Egypt: an icon, an arch manipulator and template for the femme fatale.

# WERE THE AMAZONS A REAL FIGHTING FORCE?

The Amazons were said to be a fierce female warrior race who lived and hunted on horseback at the edge of the known world. Excluding men from their ranks, they raised only daughters, who they trained in the military arts. As such, they were respected and feared: they fought the mightiest heroes from Greek legend and took part in the Trojan War. They have been memorialized on ceramics, statuary and the reliefs of temples. Are the Amazons purely mythological, or could a real army of warrior women have inspired the legends? And, has archaeology uncovered evidence of their descendants?

According to the Greek myths, the first Amazon queen was Otrera, a demigoddess born from Ares, the Greek god of war, and Harmonia, a nymph from the woods of Akmonia in Phrygia, Anatolia (in modern-day Türkiye). Otrera would go on to have four daughters with Ares: the queens Hippolyta, Penthesilea, Antiope and Melanippe. The Amazons' realm was Themiscyra, also in today's Türkiye.

As a fighting force the Amazons appeared in the myth of Bellerophon, a Corinthian hero and monster-slayer, who captured the winged horse Pegasus and killed the fire-breathing Chimera.

Bellerophon was sent on a series of quests by the Lycian king Iobates. In one task, Bellerophon took on the Amazons, who were described as fighting like men. He triumphed against these warrior women by flying on Pegasus and dropping boulders on them from above.

Similarly, one of the Twelve Labours of Heracles (Hercules) was to pit him against the Amazons. He was ordered to claim the golden belt of Ares, worn as a girdle (belt) by the Amazon Queen Hippolyta as a symbol of her authority. Heracles sailed with his crew across the Black Sea to Themiscyra and sought to win Hippolyta's girdle through seduction rather than battle. But, when a large crowd of Amazons gathered around Heracles to protect their queen, he panicked and killed Hippolyta. He took the Amazon Antiope prisoner and escaped by ship with his crew. Antiope was then presented to Theseus, King of Athens.

Amazon on horseback, Attic bell krater, 5th century BCE.

Seeking revenge, the Amazons formed an army with the Scythians and invaded Attica (an area including Athens). It took four months of conflict – the Attic War – for Theseus to finally push them back. Antiope was accidentally killed during the conflict by another Amazon named Molpadia.

There are numerous variations on most of the myths featuring the Amazons. One has Hippolyta being abducted by Theseus and giving birth to a son named Hippolytus. When Theseus then decided to marry another woman, the Amazons interrupted his wedding party and Hippolyta was mortally wounded by her sister Penthesilea.

## THE AMAZONS IN THE TROJAN WAR

The warrior women make appearances in the Trojan War as described in Homer's *Iliad* and another epic, the *Aethipois* (both *c*.8th century BCE). The sagas mention Priam, the last King of Troy, who told Helen he joined the Phrygian army in battle against the Amazons. Later, the Amazon Penthesilea, wracked with guilt for killing her sister Hippolyta, sought a noble death in battle and took Priam's coin, joining the Trojans along with 12 or more Amazons as a mercenary army, to fight against the Greeks. The Roman poet Virgil described her as 'the ferocious Penthesilea, gold belt fastened beneath her exposed breast, leads her battle-lines of Amazons with their crescent light-shields… a *bellatrix*, a maiden who dares to fight with men'.

After making quick work of a large section of the opposing Greek army, Penthesilea died at the hands of the hero Achilles. Only on removing her helmet did Achilles realize his foe was a woman. He fell in love with her (according to one version, he also abused her body) and had her buried with honours. Penthesilea was described as the last true Amazon, and her image beside the remorseful Achilles became a popular subject in classical art.

The Amazons were also encountered by the legendary Greek hero Jason and his Argonauts, who sought out the magical Golden Fleece. In Apollonius Rhodius's 3rd-century BCE version of the Argonauts' adventures, he described them as follows: 'The Amazones of the Doiantian plain were by no means gentle, well-conducted folk; they were brutal and aggressive, and their main concern in life was war. War, indeed, was in their blood, daughters of Ares as they were and of the Nymphe Harmonia, who lay with the god in the depths of the Akmonion Wood and bore him girls who fell in love with fighting.'

One dubious detail regarding the Amazons is that their name derives from the Greek *a* ('without') and *mazos* ('breast'). This idea was put forward by the Greek historian Hellanikos in the 5th century BCE. He claimed that Amazons would cut off their right breasts to improve their use of the bow and arrow. This seems a nonsensical claim: many depictions of Amazons show them displaying their intact right breasts, and having breasts does not interfere with archery. The left breast was supposedly kept intact for nursing children. More generally, to secure their female-only civilization, Amazons are said to have procreated with the men of local tribes and kept female offspring. Boys were either given away or deliberately crippled to prevent them fighting in later life. Myths about Amazonian society described men as docile and performing traditionally female roles, such as household duties and spinning wool.

While Greek legends describe the fighting prowess and culture of the Amazons, can ancient historians confirm whether they existed, and where? In the myths, the Amazons lived on the edge of the known world, or at least the wild lands east of Greece, beyond Türkiye. Heracles's quest for Hippolyta's belt took him to a river called Thermodon: today this is called the Terme and threads through Türkiye to the Black Sea.

## EARLY HISTORICAL EVIDENCE?

Thermodon is also mentioned as the location of the Amazons in the *Histories* of Herodotus, written in the 5th century BCE and regarded as the first scholarly narrative account of the ancient Greek world, though much of what it describes should be treated with some scepticism. Herodotus wrote about Greeks besting the Amazons in battle: 'after their victory on the Thermodon they sailed away carrying in three ships as many Amazons as they had been able to take alive; and out at sea the Amazons attacked the crews and killed them.' Not knowing how to sail, the Amazons arrived by accident on the shores of Scythia (the northern Black Sea coast of modern-day Ukraine and the Caucasus), where they seized horses and began raiding towns. The Scythians had their own name for the Amazons: *Oiorpata*, meaning 'killers of men'.

According to Herodotus, the Scythians managed to charm the Amazons with young men, but having married, the Amazons refused to settle like Scythian women. They argued that 'they do not have the same customs. We shoot the bow and throw the javelin and ride, but have never learned women's work; and your women do none of the things of which we speak, but stay in their wagons and do women's work, and do not go out hunting or anywhere else.' The Scythian men agreed to quit their towns and ride with the Amazons towards the river Tanaïs. (Now known as the Dnieper, this river flows from Russia through Belarus and Ukraine to the

Black Sea.) Here, the Amazons settled and continued to 'ride out hunting, with their men or without them; they go to war, and dress the same as the men'. Herodotus named their descendants as the Sauromatians (Sarmatians).

Other historians also wrote later accounts of the Amazons. The reports of the Greek historian Diodorus Siculus (1st century BCE) claimed an encounter took place between Alexander the Great and an Amazon named Thalestris, who travelled to Hyrcania (modern-day Iran) to meet 'the greatest man of that day' and 'make a baby'. This tale was thought to be invented but were the rest? While ancient Greeks and Romans seemed to have accepted the existence of the Amazons, what physical evidence do we have for them?

In the 2nd century CE, Greek-Roman chronicler Appian described the aftermath of a battle in 65BCE between the Roman general Pompey and Mithridates VI, King of Pontus (in modern-day Türkiye). Mithridates recruited both Scythians and Sarmatians for his army. Pompey won the battle and 'there were found among the prisoners and the hostages several women whose wounds were as great and as dangerous as the men. These women were said to be Amazons.' As with Herodotus, not all of the reports of Appian can be verified or trusted.

## ARMED WOMEN UNEARTHED

Excavations during the 19th and 20th centuries of burial sites on the steppes of of southern Ukraine and Russia may have found clues. These sites, called *kurgans*, are mounds of earth over wooden-framed graves. They are typical for the nomadic Scythian people who lived in the eastern European grasslands during the Iron Age, around the 4th century BCE. Inside the *kurgans*, archaeologists found the remains of women dressed in armour and with numerous weapons. Could these be the Sarmatians that Herodotus described as descendants of the Amazons and Scythians?

One of the first such graves to be uncovered included the skeleton of a female positioned in an east–west direction, with the remains of a male figure at her feet. The woman wore silver earrings, a necklace of bone and glass beads, and a bronze arm ring. The grave goods beside her included two long iron spears, a decorated wood-and-leather quiver containing knives and 47 arrowheads, plus a mirror, pottery, food and cutlery. There was no weaponry beside the male figure.

About one-fifth of the graves examined in the area around the lower rivers Don and Volga were found to contain the bodies and belongings of warrior women. The graves of warrior men were also found, but it seems female warriors were held in equal esteem. There were also graves that appeared to belong to priestesses. One grave contained the body of a girl in her early teens, along with a dagger and quiver full of arrowheads. Her bow legs suggested she had spent most of her life on horseback, while an arrowhead amulet she carried in a pouch may have signified her skills at archery.

These excavations seem to back up Herodotus's stories of a female warrior tribe being assimilated with the Scythians on the far side of the Black Sea. Whether or not these Sarmatian or Scythian women were the progeny of Amazons, it seems certain that there was a culture of fighting women that existed thousands of years ago on the Eurasian steppes. Perhaps, albeit under a different name, the Amazons lived.

The Amazons, of course, survive in another fashion. In the 16th century, when the Spanish conquistadors were exploiting

Mexico and Peru, it was thought that the Amazons might still be living as a hidden people in the South American interior. As reported by the Dominican missionary Gaspar de Carvajal, the Spanish conquistador Francesco de Orellana led a 19-month-long expedition eastwards from the coast of Peru across mountains and through jungle to explore along the Marañón river.

Eventually, de Orellana and his men came across villages where they were attacked by a small army of Indians led by tall, pale-skinned and almost naked women 'with bows and arrows in their hands, doing as much fighting as ten Indian men'. The people they encountered were the Tapuyas, for whom it was customary for the women to fight alongside the men. Surviving the encounter, and inspired by these female warriors, de Orellana renamed the Marañón river *Rio Amazonas* – the Amazon.

# WAS THERE A REAL KING ARTHUR?

The King Arthur of legend was a benevolent ancient ruler of Britain, whose circle of knights took part in noble quests and protected the country from foreign and supernatural threats. His adventures have been shared for centuries, in poems, prose and film, but are these fantastical stories based on a real character from Britain's 5th and 6th centuries? If so, who was the 'real' King Arthur?

Arthur's story, which has been embellished and altered many times, has him born in Tintagel, south-west England, the son of the British king Uther Pendragon, during a period of civil war. The young Arthur proved himself worthy of the crown by drawing a sword from a stone. Under the guidance of the wizard Merlin, Arthur claimed another enchanted sword named Excalibur from the magical Lady of the Lake.

Often these tales emphasized the chivalry and honour of a king who supposedly brought peace to Britain. His knights gathered around a Round Table at the castle of Camelot and engaged in adventures against dragons, evil knights and giants. One of their greatest exploits was the spiritual quest to find the Holy Grail, the cup used by Jesus at the Last Supper (page 182). However, there was also a dark side to the legend. The knight Lancelot had an affair with Arthur's wife Guinevere, and Arthur secretly fathered a son through incest with his sister. Their son, Mordred, joined the Round Table and plotted revenge on his father. After causing divisions between the knights, Mordred faced his father in battle. Arthur killed his son but was himself mortally wounded and his body was carried away by barge to the island of Avalon.

## ARTHUR IN HISTORICAL ACCOUNTS

Prior to the romantic legends, the earliest known mention of Arthur dates from around 828 in the *Historia Brittonum*. In this chronicle of the Britons, credited to the 9th-century Welsh monk Nennius, Arthur is described as a *dux bellorum*, or military leader, who spearheaded a Christian fight against Saxon invaders from northern Germany in the late 5th and early 6th centuries: 'Then in those days Arthur fought against them with the kings of the

Britons but he was the commander in those battles.' The validity of Nennius' work has been questioned as his tales verge on legend and may have been adapted from an earlier source. Nennius lists 12 battles, the last of which took place on Mount Badon, 'in which there fell in one day 960 men from one charge by Arthur; and no one struck them down except Arthur himself'. Historians disagree on Badon's location: sites including Dorset, Wiltshire and near Bath have been suggested.

In the 10th-century *Annales Cambrie* (*Annals of Wales*), the Battle of Badon is dated as 516: 'The Battle of Badon, in which Arthur carried the cross of our Lord Jesus Christ on his shoulders for three days and three nights and the Britons were victors.' Scholars generally agree that the battle was a real event. This decisive struggle led to a period of peace between the Britons and the Saxons, who were allowed to settle close to where they landed, on the east and south-east coasts of Britain.

Other accounts written closer to events also mention this battle, but not Arthur. These include *De Excidio et Conquestu Britanniae* (*On the Ruin and Conquest of Britain*) by the 6th-century British monk Gildas, and a 'siege of Mount Badon, when they made no small slaughter of those invaders' in the 8th-century *Ecclesiastical History of the English People* by the canonized Anglo-Saxon historian, Bede. Gildas refers to an earlier Romano-British leader known as Ambrosius Aurelianus who bears some similarity with Arthur. Mentions of Arthur can be found in medieval Welsh poetry thought to date from the 9th or 10th century. In *Y Gododdin*, one warrior is described as 'on the rampart of the stronghold, although he was no Arthur'.

The *Annales Cambrie* also provides a date and place for Arthur's death: in 537 at the Battle of Camlann, 'in which Arthur and Medraut

Statue of King Arthur by Rubin Eynon, Tintangel, Cornwall, UK.

fell; and there was plague in Britain and Ireland'. The Medraut described here is an early version of the legendary Mordred. However, there is debate over whether or not Arthur was a later addition to the annals.

More flesh was put upon Arthur's story in the chronicler and bishop Geoffrey of Monmouth's *Historia Regum Britanniae* (*History of the Kings of Britain*), written around 1136. Geoffrey described the lives of British kings from the Trojans to the Anglo-Saxon takeover. He claimed to have located a lost history of the Celts, which provided him with previously unknown details of 2,000 years of history. (This lost reference is, of course, unverified.) Among Geoffrey's more outlandish claims is that Britain was named after a Trojan called Brutus.

Geoffrey took Gildas's Ambrosius Aurelianus and transformed him into a king of Britain and the older brother of Uther

Pendragon, the future father of Arthur. The brothers are aided in battle by the wizard Merlin. Geoffrey also names Tintangel as Arthur's birthplace, and has him crowned in Caerleon-on-Usk (near modern-day Newport, Wales) aged 15. Arthur's sword, Caliburn, was said to be forged at Avalon and his castle, Camelot, located in Monmouth, Wales.

*Historia Regum Britanniae* describes Arthur successfully pushing back the Saxons, then campaigning in Ireland, Iceland, Gotland (Sweden) and Gaul (France). He brought peace to the nation but, while fighting in Gaul, Arthur's bastard nephew Mordred seduced his wife Guinevere and stole the throne. Arthur hurried back to Britain to kill Mordred but suffered a mortal injury. His body was carried away by the Nine Holy Women to the island of Avalon.

These early British 'histories' are not considered accurate by modern-day historians, with the exception of John Morris, whose 1973 book *The Age of Arthur* firmly positioned Arthur in his history of post-Roman Britain. The British medievalist David Dumville was forthright in his opinion of Arthur's inclusion, 'The fact of the matter is that there is no historical evidence about Arthur; we must reject him from our histories and, above all, from the titles of our books.'

Geoffrey of Monmouth's work incorporates some true events, however, and did much to establish the mythology of Arthur. The book was a huge hit in its time. It was translated from Latin into several other languages and over 200 manuscript copies of it have survived to the present day. King Arthur was then adopted in France, where various writers, notably Chrétien de Troyes, added elements such as the Round Table and the search for the Holy Grail.

## ARTHUR AT GLASTONBURY

The monks of Glastonbury Abbey sought to capitalize on the success of Geoffrey of Monmouth's book. When their abbey in south-west Britain suffered fire damage they needed funds for its renovation; thanks to 'strange and miraculous signs' (and, supposedly, a tip-off from King Henry II), they were led to a site in their cemetery where they conveniently discovered the remains of Arthur, buried in a hollow oak trunk with a woman beside him. As proof they presented an inscription on a lead cross, reading: 'Here lies buried the renowned King Arthur, with Guinevere his second wife, in the Isle of Avalon.' Henry II would not be the last ruler to attempt to burnish his prestige by linking his kingship to Arthur's ancient name and mystique.

These bones were reburied in a black marble tomb in front of the High Altar at Glastonbury Abbey in 1278, with King Edward I and Queen Eleanor in attendance. (The inscribed cross does not survive, although drawings exist.) Studies of the bones and the cemetery site have led experts to conclude that the remains were actually from the 7th century, and most likely the bones of a monk from the abbey. A round table was constructed in the late 13th century, possibly for a festival celebrating the engagement of one of King Edward I's daughters. It was later decorated with the image of Henry VIII and now hangs in Winchester Castle.

Legends are vague about whether Arthur was interred or taken to Avalon to recover, before returning when he is most needed, as described in Sir Thomas Malory's 15th-century epic tale, *Le Morte d'Arthur*: 'Yet some men say King Arthur is not dead but had by the will of our Lord Jesus Christ into another place; and men say he shall come again and win the holy cross. I will not say it shall be so: but many men say there is written on his tomb this verse:

"Here lies Arthur: once and future king."' Malory condensed the best elements of previous editions and chose Winchester as the site of Camelot. As one of the first titles to be printed by William Caxton in 1485, it was widely read.

In Britain's Victorian Age, Arthur and his knights were once again depicted in poetry, paintings and plays. With a resurgence in interest in the legend, new efforts were made to locate the sites described in the tales. Archaeologists sought evidence of Arthur's birth in Tintagel, and Camelot at Cadbury in Somerset. Avalon (Celtic for 'Isle of Apples') was thought to be Glastonbury Tor, once an island surrounded by marsh in centuries past. Some artefacts were discovered during these excavations. The foundations of an Iron Age fort were unearthed at Cadbury. They may not have confirmed the existence of Arthur, but they certainly kept interest alive, with tourists flocking to associated locations.

## A LIGHT IN THE DARK AGES?

While the chivalric romances contain much that is fabulous, serious academic research has attempted to trace signs of a true Arthur in Britain's 'Dark Ages' (broadly, between the end of Roman Britain in the 5th century and the Norman conquest in 1066). There is little in the written record to prove his existence. Fewer chronicles were kept after the withdrawal of the Roman armies, as remaining Romano-Britons endured civil war between clans and minor kingdoms, and regular invasions from the Danish-German Angles and German Saxons. Various names of kings or local lords appear from the mists of this time, such as Vortiporix, Cradlemas and, notably, the tyrant Vortigern (meaning 'great lord'). Vortigern is recorded as coming to an accommodation with the Saxons, bribing them with offers of land in exchange for them fighting off other enemies.

The legend of Arthur may have much earlier origins in actual events. In the 2nd century the Roman emperor Marcus Aurelius sent foreign troops to guard the northern British frontier at Hadrian's Wall against incursions by Picts from the east and north-east of modern Scotland. This unit comprised 3,000 Sarmatians from the eastern European steppes. They were garrisoned at the fort of Camboglanna (at Castlesteads near today's Carlisle); several historians have posited this as the source of the name Camlann, Arthur's final battleground. Significantly, the Sarmatians worshipped a sword in a stone and fought under a Roman officer named Lucius Artorius Castus – Artorius is the Romanized version of Arthur. Artorius's service is recorded on two inscriptions: initially a centurion, he was promoted to prefect of the Sixth Legion in York, and later commanded two legions in Europe. Could this Roman leader be the inspiration for King Arthur?

The Byzantine historian Jordanes wrote of another possible Arthur source in *The Origins and Deeds of the Goths* (*c.*551), describing a 'king of the Britons' from the late 5th century named Riothamus, who twice crossed into Gaul to quell a revolt. (Geoffrey of Monmouth's Arthur fought in Gaul, among other similarities.) One letter requesting the aid of Riothamus still exists as proof of his campaigning.

Irish and Scottish folk tales also bear some similarities to Arthurian myths. One Irish saga involves Finn Macool, a leader of hunter-warriors on various quests. Finn is killed in battle but left dormant, awaiting a future when he needs to reawaken and defend Ireland once more. In the *Life of St Columba*, written by Adomnan of Iona around 700, a prince of Dál Raida in Scotland's Clyde Valley named Artuir Mac Áedán falls in battle in 596 against a tribe known as the Miathi. Artuir's wars occur around Hadrian's Wall. Some experts believe this northern border is the setting for Arthur's adventures, rather than the south-west. Perhaps a real-life Arthur, Artuir or Artorius fought here against Picts, not Saxons.

There is a consensus among contemporary historians that Arthur was not a historical character. His knightly persona was the invention of mythologizers such as Geoffrey of Monmouth. And yet, there was and continues to be a great desire to prove that Arthur, in some form, existed. While there may not have been a war leader under that exact name, there are many such figures that could have inspired him. A country threatened with assimilation by the Saxons needed to invent a legend: a British hero to inspire the fightback. In his 1956 book, *History of the English-Speaking Peoples*, the former British prime minister Sir Winston Churchill remarked, 'if Arthur did not actually exist, he should have'.

# WAS TUTANKHAMUN MURDERED?

Undoubtedly one of the greatest archaeological finds of the 20th century, the tomb of the boy-king Tutankhamun was a wonderfully preserved trove of gold and ancient craft, and a spectacular representation of ancient Egyptian beliefs that their kings became divine after death. The 23-carat funerary mask of the young pharaoh, inlaid with coloured glass and gemstones, is now a symbol of Egypt and an international icon. But, behind the mask was the frail body still in his teens. Why did Tutankhamun die so young? Was he murdered by someone close to him?

When the British archaeologist Howard Carter entered a sealed chamber within a musty crypt in Luxor's Valley of the Kings in 1922, with his sponsor Lord Carnarvon beside him, he was the first to gaze at the wonders within for 3,244 years. Carter later wrote, 'as my eyes grew accustomed to the light, details of the room within emerged slowly from the mist, strange animals, statues, and gold – everywhere the glint of gold'. The antechamber was filled with everything a boy-king would need in the next life: ceremonial beds in the form of fantastical creatures, shrines to gods and goddesses, decorated jewellery boxes, alabaster vases, a golden throne, a chariot with archery equipment, board games and two life-size, dark-skinned statues of Tutankhamun. The treasures were piled high rather than neatly arranged, suggesting ancient tomb robbers had been disturbed, but the contents seemed to be complete. It would take Carter and his team almost ten years to catalogue the 5,398 artefacts in the chambers.

Carter alerted the Egyptian antiquities authorities and prepared for major press attention, but he was well aware the one major missing artefact was the pharaoh himself. Returning to the tomb the night before the public unveiling, Carter gouged a hole through a plaster wall between the life-size statues and crawled through. His instincts were correct. On the other side of the wall was a further chamber featuring a series of shrines and a huge stone sarcophagus with the protective images of winged goddesses (Isis, Nephthys, Neith and Selkis) cut into its corners. Another year passed before the 1.1-tonne lid of the sarcophagus was lifted: inside were three nested coffins of gilded wood decorated with precious stones, the innermost cast with more than 10 kg (22 lb) of solid gold. On 28 October 1925, using a system of pulleys, the lid of this innermost coffin was raised and the mummified remains of Tutankhamun were finally observed.

The burial chamber and stone sarcophagus of Tutankhamun, Valley of the Kings, Luxor, Egypt.

## AN INCREDIBLE AUTOPSY

Tutankhamun's head was covered with a stunning golden funerary mask adorned with the symbols of cobra and vulture goddesses, representing Upper and Lower Egypt. Around his throat was a collar of glass and semi-precious stones. The wrapped figure was blackened from the liberal use of tar-like embalming fluids that effectively glued him to the bottom of the coffin. The body, in its coffin, was carried into the sunlight and experts called in to help unwrap it. Heated paraffin wax was poured over the outer layer of bandages so they could be sliced into and removed as one piece when cool. Tucked between the bandages were 143 amulets and items of jewellery. The process of unwrapping and documenting these layers took more than 18 months. Once uncovered, the body was revealed to be in a poor state and could not be cut free from its coffin. Douglas Derry, professor of anatomy at Cairo University, took the decision to cut the mummy so that it could be autopsied.

The pharaoh was measured at 167 cm (5.5 ft) tall. Based on the bones, Derry calculated Tutankhamun's age at death as between 18 and 20. An early opinion was that the boy-king had died from tuberculosis. Decades before CAT scans and DNA tests, methods used to investigate ancient corpses were fairly destructive and after 33 centuries, Tutankhamun's body was brittle. The Egyptian Antiquities Services decided to leave Tutankhamun in his tomb and it wasn't until 1969 that a portable X-ray machine was able to scan the body.

A team led by R.G. Harrison, an anatomist from the University of Liverpool, made individual X-rays of Tutankhamun's head and limbs, and found he was missing part of his sternum and ribs. Was this the result of a chest injury or damage done during mummification? Studies of the spine allowed Harrison to rule out tuberculosis as the cause of death, but the skull X-rays gave the team pause for thought. At the base of the skull was a dense area that Harrison thought could have been caused by a haemorrhage resulting from a blow to the back of the head. This dark area on the X-ray could also have been where resin was introduced into the cranium during the gory mummification process, and welled inside the skull. The X-rays also showed a loose bone fragment inside the skull; however, this sat above the resin, so it was likely that it broke free after Tutankhamun's death and mummification, perhaps during the violent removal of the body from the coffin. Harrison believed this fragment was part of the ethmoid bone in the sinuses that broke off when Tutankhamun's embalmers used a hooked tool to break into the skull and remove the brain.

Later examinations of the X-rays by Dr Gerald Irwin, head of radiology at Winthrop University Hospital, USA, reconfirmed the initial conclusion that a blow to the head caused a blood clot – an injury that Tutankhamun could have survived for several weeks, perhaps in a coma, but which could have also caused his death. Was this blow an accident, or a deliberate act by an enemy or rival of the young pharaoh? If Tutankhamun had been murdered, who could have dealt the blow or ordered the assassination attempt?

## THE UNUSUAL SUSPECTS

When Tutankhamun came to power around 1332BCE, he was married to his half-sister Ankhesenamun. There is evidence that he died unexpectedly in 1322BCE. His tomb in the Valley of the Kings was incomplete, so a non-royal tomb was appropriated and decorated over 70 days while Tutankhamun's body underwent the elaborate mummification process. Many of the treasures placed in his tomb seem to have been altered, with faces, text and cartouches being replaced, suggesting they may have been unfinished, or taken from other tombs. Visible soldering marks suggest Tutankhamun's famous golden burial mask may also have been repurposed.

Tutankhamun had no obvious successor, so two chief advisers who took power after his death – his vizier, Ay, and his general, Horemheb – are obvious suspects if there was a plot to murder the boy king. Ankhesenamun feared she would be forced to marry one of these 'commoners': she even appealed in writing to Suppiluliuma, ruler of Egypt's enemy, the Hittites, to provide a royal husband for her. He sent his son, Prince Zannanza to Egypt, but the prince was killed at the border.

Ankhesenamun now had no choice but to marry the elderly advisor Ay, but having legitimized his claim to the throne she promptly disappeared from the record. While she is depicted on the throne and wall of Tutankhamun's tomb, she is absent from Ay's tomb and her burial place has never been discovered. Was Ankhesenamun killed along with Tutankhamun and Prince Zannanza? Ay is depicted in Tutankhamun's tomb already wearing a pharaoh's crown while performing his duties as a priest. Ay would later claim Tutankhamun's original unfinished tomb for himself. Horemheb, meanwhile, must have been alerted to Prince Zannanza's journey to the border and could have ordered his assassination. He followed Ay and claimed the throne of Egypt from 1319 to 1292BCE. Did the two work together to grasp the reins of power?

Howard Carter had his own suspicions, noting: '…it was Ay who was largely responsible for establishing the boy king upon the throne. Quite possibly he had designs upon it himself already, but, not feeling secure enough for the moment, preferred to bide his time and utilize the opportunities he would undoubtedly have, as minister to a young and inexperienced sovereign, to consolidate his position.'

## A HIGH-RISK HOBBY

The theory that Tutankhamun was a murder victim killed with a blunt instrument endured for decades, until CT (computed tomography) scans of the mummy were made in 2005 by an

Egyptian-led research team. These scans produce images of soft tissue as well as bone, providing a detailed three-dimensional image of the subject. As reported by Egypt's top archaeologist, Zahi Hawass, the CT scans of Tutankhamun showed there was no evidence of an attack. In addition, damage to his chest area was caused after his death. The studies produced fresh claims that Tutankhamun had bone necrosis and a club foot. The boy-king may have needed to use a cane to move about; 130 canes were found in his tomb, although these were also carried as a sign of status. Genetic tests also found traces of malaria.

In particular, the scan discovered an ancient fracture on the king's left thigh bone. As embalming fluid had seeped into the fracture, and there was no sign of repair, this appeared to be an injury sustained close to the time of death. A new hypothesis was suggested, that Tutankhamun died as the result of injuries in a hunting accident. The chariot and archery set in his tomb was evidence of his love of the sport. Young kings would often chase after ostriches in the desert east of Heliopolis, the seat of worship of the sun god Aten. (As king, Tutankhamun was proclaimed as the 'living image of Aten'.) A golden ostrich-feather fan found in Tutankhamun's burial chamber, close to the king, bore an inscription that claimed the 42 feathers in the fan were taken from ostriches that he caught. A 'virtual autopsy' of Tutankhamun was undertaken by a team led by Dr Chris Naunton of the Egypt Exploration Society in 2013, using the X-ray and CT data of his body. Naunton came to the conclusion that the pharaoh was killed in a chariot crash during a hunting party and the wound on his chest caused by a kick from a horse.

While some may have had motives for an attempt on Tutankhamun's life, in the light of modern scientific analysis it seems the most probable reason for the young pharaoh's death was an injury while hunting – his leg was broken and this was followed by a severe case of malaria. The fact that his heart, considered by ancient Egyptians to be the source of reasoning, was not included in the canoptic jars in Tutankhamun's tomb suggests it was too decayed to be removed from his body intact and that the body had taken time to reach the embalmer's table, perhaps from the hunting ground.

Most of the few records of Tutankhamun's reign were erased by his successors and there is no ancient report of his death. Autopsies have revealed many signs of disease and frailty, but unfortunately nothing is conclusive. The mystery of Tutankhamun's final days only adds to the allure of this glittering young king.

# CHAPTER 5
# RITUAL TRACES

Over a thousand years ago, the indigenous people of South America etched enigmatic shapes and straight lines into the landscape. These ancient traces are on a colossal scale, crossing hundreds of miles of open land. While Peru's Nazca Lines may be the most famous example, the Sajama Lines in Bolivia cover even more ground. Only properly mapped 50 years ago, this web of sacred footpaths and prehistoric debris invites much investigation. Were they meant to be seen by gods? There are theories too that Britain is criss-crossed with ancient paths that link significant spiritual sites and these 'ley lines' convey some kind of supernatural energy. Were the people that planned them trying to communicate with spirits or was there ritual attached to walking them? On Costa Rica's jungle terrain some 300 mammoth stone spheres were arranged in lines. Sculpted from boulders over 1,000 years ago, and weighing up to 15 tonnes, the spheres would have required phenomenal effort to shape and locate. The culture that placed them is long gone. Will we ever know their significance?

# WHAT WAS THE PURPOSE OF THE NAZCA LINES?

Around 2,000 years ago, the indigenous people of Peru dug patterns in the dry soil of the Nazca Desert, forming 1,300 km (800 miles) of intersecting pathways, geometric shapes and images of animals and plants on a massive scale that can only be fully appreciated from the sky. Why did these ancient people sketch these geoglyphs, all kilometres long, and what did the shapes and patterns mean: were they invitations to gods or other visitors from the skies?

The indigenous Nazca people hailed from a group of minor kingdoms that thrived between 1CE and 700. They were farmers and fishers who also produced high quality pottery and textiles. The decorations on their pots and cloth are of similar humans, animals and plants as those drawn at scale in the desert, 400 km (250 miles) south-east of Lima.

The first written record of these 'Nazca Lines' was within *La Chronica del Peru*, a history provided by the Spanish conquistador Pedro Cieza de Léon in 1553. He described the lines as trail markers: 'and in some parts of the desert are seen signs, so that they [the Indians] find the path that has to be taken'. A decade later, a man named Luis Monzón recorded that locals said they were roads made by past generations of the Inca.

More accurate descriptions began to emerge during the 1920s–30s, initially when the Peruvian archaeologist Toribio Mejía Xesspe publicly shared his discovery of long, straight lines in the desert that could be seen from neighbouring hills. Peruvian military pilots reported sighting the lines, but they were barely investigated. The first proper studies of the lines took place after 1940 when Paul Kosok, a history professor from New York's Long Island University, flew over the Nazca Desert and identified the large image of a bird.

He began to map out the shapes and work out how the lines were made, together with American archaeologist Richard P. Schaedel and German-Peruvian mathematician Maria Reiche. (Nicknamed the 'Lady of the Lines', Reiche would spend decades studying and preserving the Nazca Lines.) The 40 or so figures the team found on the desert surface included a hummingbird, condor, monkey, tarantula, dog, orca, llamas and several plants. There were also geometric shapes and spiral patterns. One spiral was made of parallel lines, forming a circle 90 m (300 ft) in diameter. Near its centre, Reiche found an upright stone inscribed with an image of a snake and severed head. Perhaps the spirals represented serpents.

The l34 m- (440 ft)-long image of a condor etched into the Nazca Desert, Peru.

## AN AMAZING CREATIVE FEAT

The lines were created by digging a narrow trench 10–15 cm (4–6 in) deep. This removed the top layer of reddish pebbles from the surface to reveal paler earth below. The discovery of wooden poles near the lines indicated that the people of Nazca marked out the lines in advance of digging trenches, to make sure the paths remained straight when desired. It has been suggested they may have woven cotton hot-air balloons to allow them to direct the giant drawings from above, although this is unlikely.

Later, archaeologists attempted to calculate when the lines were made by noting where they crossed over earlier paths and by carbon-dating the posts used in their construction. This led to estimates that the Nazca Lines were prepared between 500BCE and 500CE. The lines are well preserved thanks to the relatively dry, windless climate of the desert. The effort and planning involved in drawing these geoglyphs was immense. The largest figures have been measured at nearly 370 m (1,200 ft) in area. The famous hummingbird figure alone is 93 m (305 ft) long.

The more perplexing and lasting mystery is why the Nazca people went to such incredible lengths. In June 1941, a day after the winter solstice and while he was at ground level in the desert, Paul Kosok witnessed the sun dipping exactly where the lines were converging on the horizon. This led to him describing the network of lines in the desert as 'the largest astronomy book in the world'. Both Kosok and Reiche suggested the patterns acted to mark particular dates where the sun and other celestial bodies would appear.

Reiche later proposed that the lines represented constellations; she argued the image of a long-tailed monkey showed the Great

Bear constellation that may have helped to mark the passage of time and season changes. Alternatively, in 1977, the priest and historian Alberto Rossel Castro thought the lines might be related to irrigation routes or the division of plots of land. The Canadian archaeologist Persis Clarkson followed 1,600 km (1,000 miles) of the lines and unearthed potsherds (broken ceramics), the foundations of basic shelters and cairns along her route. In her report published in 1990, she said she believed the lines could have been walked and swept as part of some religious cleansing ritual.

## A TOOL TO SIGNAL ALIENS OR TALK TO GODS?

Of the more far-fetched explanations for the Nazca Lines, the Swiss writer Erich von Däniken theorized in his 1968 book *Chariots of the Gods* that the lines were designed as landing strips for extraterrestrial visitors. One simplistic humanoid image with rounded eyes in the desert has been given the name 'The Astronaut', although this may be a primitive image of a fisher.

More realistically, in 1985 the American archaeologist Johan Reinhard presented historic evidence that the Nazca people worshipped mountains and water sources and claimed that the giant figures were part of that worship in aid of healthy crop production. He noted that some churches and villages in neighbouring Bolivia were joined by similar 'sacred' lines (see pages 232–3). The Nazca Lines are not wide enough for groups to walk together side by side. Instead people passing within the boundaries would have walked in a line, like a procession, adding weight to the idea that the paths were used for religious rituals. It has also been noted that the animal shapes were drawn using one single line that does not cross itself. These images too could have been walked as part of a continuous route.

The ancient ceremonial capital of the Nazca people was at Cahauchi, a series of mounds and platforms above the flood plain of the Nazca River. Here they erected a 'Great Temple' pyramid, 21 m (70 ft) high and made of mudbrick, among other buildings and squares. The skulls of numerous severed heads have been found at the site. Cahauchi does not appear to include residential buildings; it seems to have been used solely for rituals, including sacrifices.

Currently, the most widely held belief among archaeologists and historians is that the Nazca Lines were prepared as part of walking rituals to allow the Nazca people to communicate with the gods so they would deliver water for crops. The animal images could be related to spirit beings, particularly those associated with water and fertility. One could imagine processions travelling along the lines to the sounds of chanting, drums and panpipes, keeping the path clear with their movement, or else a single shaman, communicating with the mountain and water gods, asking for rain. The plateau where the lines are drawn is bone dry, but rain does fall on the neighbouring Nazca hills, feeding the rivers and streams through the valleys. The lines, patterns and animal images could be intended to draw the attention of the gods and bring life-giving waters to the arid desert.

In recent years, international and Peruvian teams of archaeologists have used drone and AI technology to survey the area. Their work has added to the number of geoglyphs recorded in the region, producing a new total of over 360. The nearby town of Palpa has its own, possibly even older geoglyphs, of mostly human and animal figures. And these are far from the only such ancient marks.

## WHO WALKED THE SAJAMA LINES?

Forming a web over western Bolivia's Altiplano, in the shadow of the Nevado Sajama volcano, the country's highest point, are thousands of straight paths. Many bisect other lines. These lines were etched, perhaps more than 3,000 years ago, by the indigenous people of the high plateau. Known as the Sajama Lines, they were created in a similar way to the Nazca Lines but are even greater in scale, covering an area of 22,525 sq km (8,697 square miles), or about 15 times bigger. While the Sajama Lines are only 1–3 m (3–10 ft) in width, they extend for up to 20 km (12 miles) and walking the total distance these paths cover would mean hiking for about 16,000 km (10,000 miles).

The first modern, though brief, mention of the lines is found in the Swiss-born Argentinian adventurer Aimé Felix Tschiffely's account of his travels on horseback from Buenos Aires to New York over three years from 1925. Soon after, scholars began to take notice. It is thought that the lines were scored into the ground in pre-Columbian times, possibly before the Inca civilization took over this part of Bolivia. The anthropologist Alfred Metraux included details of the lines in his work on the indigenous people of the Carangas region, an ethnic group that lived in the southern Altiplano from about 1000 to 1476. They built fortified settlements on hilltops close to water and may have farmed, but probably relied more on herding camelids for meat and wool. The Carangas may have created and used the lines for pilgrimages, evidenced by a number of shrines (*wak'as*) and burial towers (*chullpas*) placed along several lines. There were also small settlements, perhaps used as resting points for pilgrims making a long journey.

Following the arrival of the Spanish colonists in the 16th century, many Carangas were forced to work in silver mines.

Despite efforts to convert them to Christianity, many continued to practise their pre-Columbian rituals and walk the Sajama Lines; however, Catholic churches appeared in hilltop settlements that were end-points for some lines, and stone shrines were built along the paths. Public awareness of the lines increased in the 1970s after the British writer and filmmaker Tony Morrison produced a documentary and books on the subject.

Concern that these vast and ancient traces might be erased through tourism and ignorance led to the Landmarks Foundation setting up a Tierra Sajama project (2008), with the backing of the University of Pennsylvania. They created a computer map of the lines for research and to encourage their preservation. As a major tourist attraction already, there are also concerns about the Nazca and Sajama Lines being altered or worn away by visitors. More threatening to all of these ancient routes is the possibility of changing weather patterns due to local deforestation and climate change. The lines are shallow and could be washed away by flooding or covered by mudslides. The site of the Sajama Lines, the Altiplano, is now a national park and a protected area, while the Nazca plain is today a Unesco world heritage site and protected, one hopes, for generations to ponder the significance of these awe-inspiring signals to the skies.

# WAS ÖTZI THE ICEMAN A MURDER VICTIM?

On a hiking trip across the Ötztaler Alps on the Austrian–Italian border in September 1991, Helmut and Erika Simon were shocked to discover part of a body protruding from the ice below them. The body was 3,210 m (10,530 ft) above sea level on the Hauslabjoch Pass. It was a warm summer and much of the ice on the high pass had melted, so the hikers assumed the frozen figure had recently fallen from the mountain and died due to cold weather. In fact, they were millennia out in their assumption. Once removed from the ice, the mummified figure, who would be named Ötzi after the region where he was recovered, was identified as being 5,000 years old. What's more, he did not appear to have been killed by a fall. The hikers had unwittingly opened the files on what seemed to be an ancient murder mystery.

The manager of the mountain rescue centre the hikers called after spotting the body alerted Italian and Austrian police. They arrived at the site the following day and began cutting the body from its position in a hollow beneath a glacier. Fifty years earlier, an Italian music professor had gone missing in the area and the excavators thought these were his remains. Then they saw tatters of animal-skin clothing and an axe with an iron blade.

By a stroke of luck, the famous mountaineers Reinhold Messner (who made the first successful solo ascent of Mount Everest) and Han Kammerlander, along with their local guide Kurt Fritz, were touring the region. They looked at a drawing of Ötzi's axe, and

Messner estimated its age as between 500 and 3,000 years old. They climbed up the pass to see the body in situ. More of the figure was now visible: the head appeared to have been smashed in, and there seemed to be evidence of whipping and burning on the skin.

Messner was knowledgeable about archaeology and the area's history. In a press interview he suggested the 'iceman' was once a mercenary in the army of 'Frederick Empty-Purse', a 15th-century Tyrolean count. If so, the wounds that were becoming visible on the body could have been inflicted by an enemy army.

Four days after its discovery, the body of the iceman was finally released from the ice and airlifted to the Institute of Forensic Medicine in Innsbruck, Austria. Preliminary checks suggested the body was that of a man about 40 years old who had died of exposure rather than his arrow wound. The skull was not broken from an attack and the supposed whip marks on his lower back, left leg, right ankle and knee were revealed as tattoos made using a pigment mixed from soot.

Konrad Spindler, professor of archaeology at Innsbruck University, examined the body and effects. He thought the axe might be bronze and suggested the body was 4,000 years old. This was confirmed by radiocarbon dating of frozen grass around the body, which placed Ötzi as living between 2,600 and 2,900BCE. Further tests undertaken by three laboratories gave him an age of 5,200 years, older than the Egyptian pyramids.

He was thought to be 160 cm (5 ft 3 in) tall when alive and to have weighed about 50 kg (110 lb). Analysis of pollen grains and his tooth enamel allowed experts to pinpoint his origin. Ötzi apparently grew up in the South Tyrol, before moving to live in valleys only about 50 km (30 miles) further north. It appears that he did not venture any further than 60 km (37 miles) from his birthplace. From his stomach contents, scientists were able to deduce that he fed on ibex, chamois and deer meat, along with einkorn wheat, nuts and fruits. Scientists were even able to tell that he ate his last meal just two hours before his death.

Thorough archaeological study of the site where Ötzi was found uncovered belongings including a patched jacket made of deerskin, a bearskin hood with a leather chin strap, fur leggings, a leather apron, shoes stuffed with grass, a cloak made from woven grasses, a goat-fur rucksack, a net, a birch-bark beaker, a stone pendant, a fire-making kit, and a bow and quiver holding 12 arrows with flint arrowheads. The axe was found to be fashioned from copper attached to a yew handle. Ötzi's bow and arrows were incomplete. This could indicate that he was not fully prepared for a hunting trip and may instead have carried these tools as part of his role as a shepherd, to protect his flock and hunt wild game for food. His tattoos and beaded pendant led some experts to argue that he was not just a hunter or shepherd but a shaman of some kind.

Despite tests showing Ötzi was of ancient pedigree, a woman from Zurich stepped forward to claim the iceman was her father, a resourceful man who had disappeared on a climbing trip in the 1970s. She was convinced he could have survived for some time by fashioning similar primitive tools and clothing.

While studies continued in Innsbruck, a row broke out over whether Austria or Italy 'owned' the world's oldest preserved hunter. Italian officials claimed that Austrian specialists were failing to adequately preserve the body; indeed, fungus had begun to sprout on Ötzi's skin. The border between the countries was obscured by snow, but it was later confirmed that Ötzi had lain on the Italian side by just 90 m (300 ft). An agreement was made that

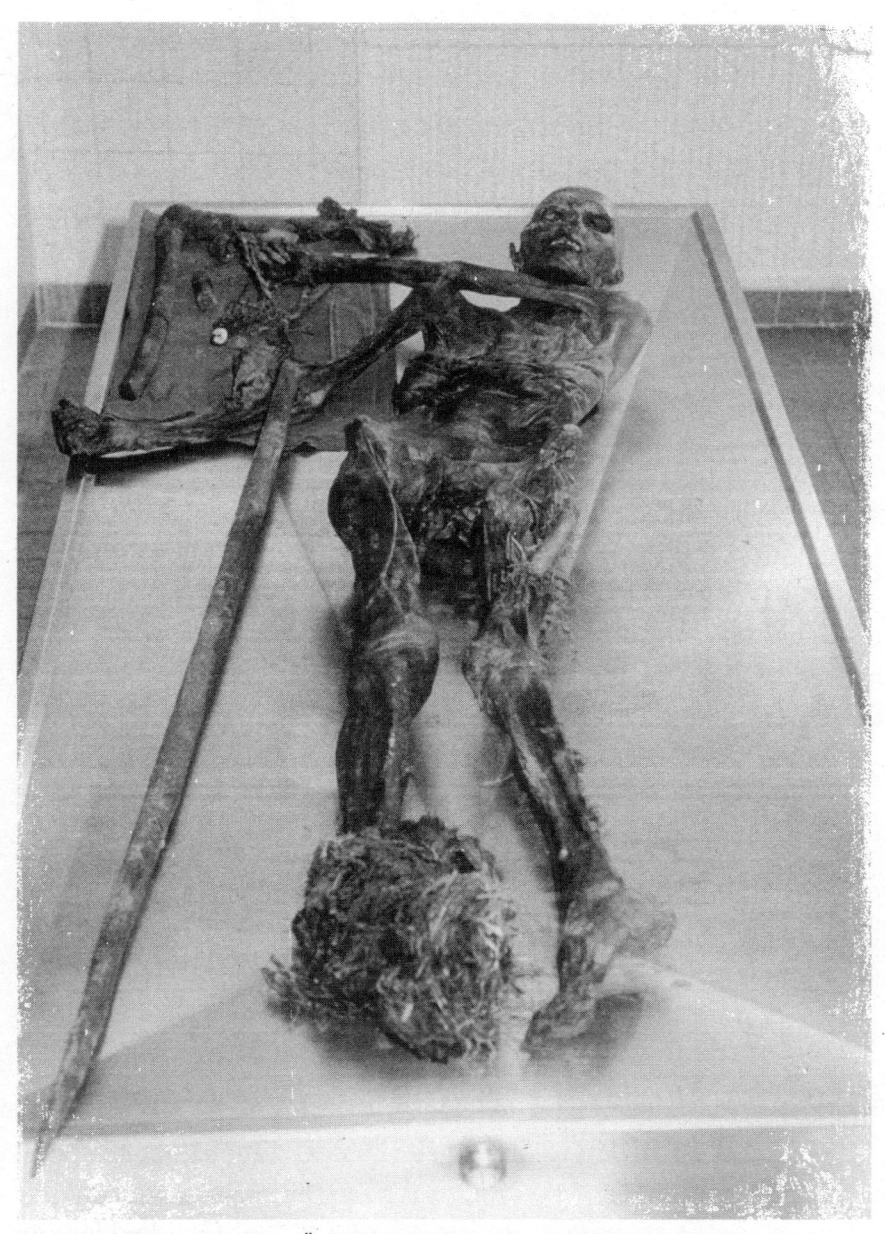

The mummified remains of Ötzi the Iceman at the Institute of Legal Medicine, Innsbruck.

allowed Austrian scientists to continue examining the body, before returning it to Italy for display in 1998.

Another controversy around the iceman hit the headlines when it was claimed that semen had been found in Ötzi's anus, making him the world's earliest-known homosexual. The story turned out to be a hoax perpetrated by an Australian magazine. It was also speculated that Ötzi's penis had been removed at some point. If true, this could indicate he was part of some kind of prehistoric self-mutilation cult; however, this was also proven to be another rumour. The iceman's genitals were intact, just reduced to a few centimetres in length by age and cold.

As well as this rather intrusive discussion of Ötzi's sexual orientation and manhood, there have been several claims that the iceman himself is a hoax: a mummy transported to the glacier in more recent times. Photographic, film and radiocarbon evidence clearly disputes such claims.

Another strange suggestion arising from the discovery of Ötzi is that those connected with his remains were cursed. Helmut Simon, one of the hikers who discovered Ötzi, disappeared in the Alps in 2004. He was not found for eight days due to snowy conditions; only an hour after Simon's funeral, the head of the mountain rescue team assigned to find him died of a heart attack. Rainer Henn, a scientist from Innsbruck University who placed Ötzi's frozen remains into a body bag, died in a car crash on his way to give a lecture on the iceman one year afterwards. Kurt Fritz, a mountaineer who led Henn to the iceman's body, died in an avalanche in 1993. And finally, Rainer Hoelzl, an Austrian journalist who filmed Ötzi's removal from the mountain, died of a brain tumour shortly after finishing his film. Of course, these events are probably coincidental, especially as mountain life involves a certain level of risk. Hundreds of other people were associated with the collection and study of Ötzi's remains, most of whom led a long and healthy life.

The publication of Ötzi's genetic information has revealed a wealth of detail on his appearance while alive. He had dark hair and eyes, plus tan skin similar to that seen in southern Italy. Although locally born, he was descended from Anatolian farmers (from modern-day Türkiye). Ötzi was not in the best of health before he was caught in wintry conditions. Three or four of his ribs showed signs of fracture, perhaps due to the weight of ice on his frame, or from an accident or attack prior to his death. He suffered from arthritis and exhibited the earliest-recorded signs of Lyme disease, an bacterial infection transmitted by ticks. Examination of his fingernails showed their growth was interrupted at least three times by serious illness during the six months prior to his death. The contents of his colon revealed he had an intestinal parasite that could have given him chronic diarrhoea. Injured and in discomfort, the poor hunter had been unlucky to end up in an exposed area during an unseasonal storm.

And what about the cause of Ötzi's death? Scans performed in 2001 revealed an arrowhead embedded in his left shoulder. The arrow also caused a tear in his coat and the shaft appeared to have been broken off. There were also signs of bruising and deep cuts on his hands and chest, plus indications of a blow to the head. It is thought that the main cause of Ötzi's death was blood loss from the arrow wound.

In 2003, a team of researchers from Australia studied DNA samples from his tools and clothing and found evidence of blood from four individuals – on an arrow, the knife blade and Ötzi's coat. They presented a scenario in which Ötzi was involved in a border dispute and wounded about 48 hours before his death, but able to use his arrows to kill two attackers. He was eventually brought down by an arrow himself. Another hypothesis had Ötzi killed as part of a ritual sacrifice.

However he died, Ötzi's body was quickly covered up during an early autumn blizzard (as dated by pollen). This prevented his body from being infested by insect larvae before it was covered with further snow and ice. The conditions effectively freeze-dried him and his belongings.

Ötzi's remains and belongings are on display at the South Tyrol Museum of Archaeology in Bolzano, Italy, where they are kept in a specially designed cold cell and are viewable through a small window – an opportunity to peer 5,000 years back in time. Ötzi lived a hard life that ended unfortunately, but we are lucky that he was preserved through a series of flukes. While we may never know exactly why he died, his poor, battered body and all of his accoutrements have opened up a window on a time five millennia ago that science has been able to embellish with incredible detail.

# WHAT IS THE MEANING OF THE DIQUÍS SPHERES?

Like rocky pearls cast to the ground by some Central American god, the Diquís Spheres are bizarre additions to the lush environment of Costa Rica. Three hundred of these *bolas de piedra* (stone balls) have been found on the Diquís Delta and on Isla del Caño, about 30 km (19 miles) offshore. These boulders were smoothed into near-perfect globes: there are no chisel marks, no inscriptions, and no pictorial reliefs to provide a clue about how, and more importantly why, they were sculpted.

The spheres were found in the south of Costa Rica, in an area known as the Diquís Delta in Puntarenas province. They were discovered in 1939, when the United Fruit Company was clearing a jungle to make way for a banana plantation. Thinking little of them at first, workers shoved aside the stones their bulldozers were unearthing from thick layers of sediment. There were rumours that spheres hidden in the jungle contained gold, so some workmen returned later with tools and drilled into some of the balls, even trying to blow them up with dynamite. All this did was crack or split the balls, and no riches came tumbling out of their centres.

Luckily, before many more were broken apart the American archaeologist Doris Stone, who was the daughter of a United Fruit executive and later the director of Costa Rica's National Museum, came to investigate. The results of her studies were published in 1943 in the journal *American Antiquity*, where they drew the attention of fellow American archaeologist and photographer, Samuel Kirkland Lothrop from Harvard University's Peabody Museum. Lothrop's own reports were published in 1963. He measured the spheres and mapped out their positions. He found one group near Jalaca containing 45 balls in total and of the 186 spheres he mapped, just 50 were thought to be in their original positions. Before their historic worth was realized, many of the smaller and medium-sized spheres were taken and used as garden and park ornaments. By one estimate, 95 per cent of the stone balls were removed from their original setting.

Stone spheres of the Diquís, Costa Rica.

Over 300 of these stone spheres have now been located. Most of the spheres are cut from gabbro, a coarse-grained igneous rock related to basalt, sourced from a few kilometres away. Around two dozen are either limestone or sandstone. They range in size from 70 cm (27 in) across to massive globes at 2.57 m (8.4 ft) in diameter that weigh up to 13.5 tonnes.

There are, unsurprisingly, legends explaining how the stones came to be placed in the jungles of Costa Rica. According to one local myth, the indigenous people had a magical potion that could soften the rock enough for them to shape it. The indigenous Bribri people from eastern Costa Rica refer to the spheres as 'Tara's cannonballs'. Tara or Tlatchque is their god of thunder, who used a giant blowpipe to fire the stone balls at the Serkes, gods of winds and hurricanes, to repel them from the Costa Rican lands.

With no handy magical potion, and certainly no metal tools to chisel rock into globes, whoever fashioned the spheres would have had to use other rocks to cut into rounded boulders before smoothing them with sand. The stone used for most of the spheres has been shown to lose layers when subjected to sudden changes in temperature, so stones could have been given a roughly rounded shape by heating them over hot coals, then applying cold water. It's estimated that to produce just one of the smaller spheres would have occupied a worker for a minimum of two weeks. This work was probably done at the initial quarry site, as the finished ball could then be more easily rolled into position.

The Diquís spheres have proved difficult to date because they have been moved from their original quarried position. They can't be dated according to their surrounding soil layers and, without organic content, they can't be radiocarbon-dated either. They are believed to have been shaped by the now-extinct pre-Columbian Diquís culture that thrived in the area between 700 and 1530CE. Some say they are a natural phenomenon. In the 1998 book *Atlantis in America: Navigators of the Ancient World* authors Ivar Zapp and George Erikson suggested the spheres were 12,000 years old and had been transported from the mythical lost island of Atlantis (page 13); these claims have been treated with scepticism.

Samuel Kirkland Lothrop's excavations found pottery in the soil below one sphere that he thought typical of the Aguas Buenas culture that lived in the area between 200BCE and 600CE. He also uncovered the broken head of a painted human statuette beneath one sphere. Based on similar finds, he dated this to 1000–1500CE.

The indigenous Diquís culture first appeared in the Valley of the Rio Grande de Térraba, and its people settled in small farming communities ruled by a regional chief. The Diquís cultivated maize, manioc, beans, squash, avocado and other tropical fruits. During the Aguas Buenas Period they were trading goods with neighbouring tribes and carving stone into cylinder shapes and figures. It is thought that the large spheres were shaped during this period and aligned with pebbled public squares or placed beside pathways leading to the homes of their chieftains.

By the Chiriquí Period (800–1550), the Diquís settlements were town-sized communities, with around a thousand inhabitants. Their largest structures were built using rounded boulders. At one site of spheres, two mounds with pebble retaining walls have been found, along with a cemetery. Many spheres appear to have been deliberately placed beside an entrance ramp to one raised building. While stone spheres are not unique to Costa Rica – individual spheres from the early Maya period have been discovered in Mexico and Guatemala – nowhere else on Earth have stone spheres of this size and number been found at archaeological sites.

This leaves the fundamental question of the stone spheres' significance to the people that crafted them. Unfortunately, there are no written records to interpret. Perhaps the most obvious theory is that the spheres represent planets in various states of movement and phase in the heavens. Melissa Rudin Hernández, a Costa Rican architect who has studied how indigenous cultures viewed the cosmos, argued the spheres symbolized the creation of the universe. John Hoopes, of the University of Kansas, who worked to award Unesco World Heritage protection for the spheres believed, 'the making and moving of the balls was probably an important social activity, perhaps more important than possession of the finished product…We believe that the balls may have sat in front of the houses of prominent people, perhaps as a display of power, of esoteric knowledge, or of control over labor.'

It has also been suggested that the spheres provided an astronomical calendar, marking celestial events such as the solstice.

Unfortunately, due to the relocation of most of the spheres checking their alignment with stars and planets is no longer possible. Others believe there are ancient manuscripts hidden within the spheres; as the Diquís Spheres are now a Unesco World Heritage Site, they are protected from further interference.

Some of the smaller stone balls were found in burial mounds, so perhaps these represented individual wealth or status. Some were buried in open ground. According to the American archaeolgist Dr Tim McGuinness, who studied the spheres for more than 30 years, numerous small spheres could have acted as route markers through what was once dense forest, especially if brightly painted. Some spheres that came into private hands were examined by McGuinness and found to have residual traces of a lime coating that would have given the sphere a white finish.

The Diquís culture died out centuries ago. Accounts from 1570, following an expedition by the conquistador Perafán de Ribera, claimed that the Diquís people had either abandoned their settlements or died, perhaps from the infectious diseases brought over from Europe by the Spanish colonizers.

The *bolas de piedra* remain an enigma. While not understood, they have been adopted as symbols of Costa Rica, even appearing on stamps. The spheres also inspired the opening sequence to the 1981 movie *Raiders of the Lost Ark*. The broken stones dynamited by plantation workers have been reassembled and exhibited in the National Museum of Costa Rica in San José. Several others have been placed outside the capital's Legislative Assembly building, where visitors can ponder their meaning and marvel at the ingenuity and purposefulness of a people long disappeared into history.

# DO LEY LINES EXIST?

Over a century ago, Alfred Watkins paused on his journey across Herefordshire, a county in western England on the border with Wales, to consult his map. As a photographer, he had a keen eye and interest in the landscape, so he was familiar with many of its most ancient sites. Suddenly, he was struck by the detail that several hilltop ruins could be connected with a straight line. The more Watkins looked into this, the more he was convinced that ancient sites had been deliberately placed to line up, and that the English landscape was crossed with mysterious ancient pathways he called 'ley lines'. Was Watkins right, and did some spiritual energy draw our prehistoric predecessors to shape and follow these direct routes?

Born in Hereford in 1855, Watkins began to photograph hills, ancient trees and archaeological sites as he travelled for his family's business. It was on a visit to the village of Blackwardine that he had his revelation about ley lines. From then on, he set about mapping alignments between sites of interest. In September 1921, he shared his theories at a meeting of the Woolhope Naturalists' Field Club (still active today), before publishing *Early British Trackways* in 1922 and a more comprehensive account, *The Old Straight Track*, in 1925.

Watkins' ideas, as he first presented them, involved the existence of prehistoric trading routes that followed straight lines between significant sites or 'mark points', particularly those on hills that could be seen from a great distance. He chose the word *ley* from the Old English for cleared space.

Archaeologists found Watkins' theory of ley lines to be preposterous, dismissing as foolish the idea that trade routes would have gone over peaks rather than around them. The archaeologist O.G.S. Crawford, who was also editor of the leading British archaeological magazine *Antiquity*, filed correspondence on the subject in a 'Crankeries' folder and even refused to accept an advertisement for Watkins' book. Watkins himself expressed some uncertainty, at least early on. In the introduction to *The Old Straight Track*, he noted that his book was asking 'whether it is a humanly designed fact, an accidental coincidence, or a "mare's nest" that mounds, moats, beacons, and mark stones fall into straight lines throughout Britain, with fragmentary evidence of trackways on the alignments'.

## LEY LINE HUNTING GAINS GROUND

Despite scholarly scepticism, Watkins' ideas found an eager audience with the wider public, and many amateur antiquarians began seeking ley lines. They found numerous occasions of at least four sites of historical interest and standing stones aligned on straight paths, seeing this as proof of the theory. Watkins encouraged these enthusiasts further by publishing *The Ley Hunter's Manual* in 1927.

Later ley hunters began to ascribe more spiritual justifications for the laying of pathways that Watkins had seen mainly as trading or ceremonial routes. From the 1960s, ideas about the lines possessing 'cosmic energy' became widespread. Rather than simply placing sites along easy-to-follow straight lines, the suggestion was that Neolithic people had been drawn by a site's spiritual energy that connected them with the Earth or cosmos in some fashion.

Some people used dowsing, an unscientific method following the movement of loosely held rods, to detect this energy.

## ARGUMENTS AGAINST 'LEYS'

There are numerous problems with Watkins' theory of ley lines. One is that the sheer number of historic sites, particularly in southern England, makes it possible to draw a multitude of straight lines on the map and cross several landmarks with ease. Watkins' lines also incorporated sites from different eras and of varying significance, such as Neolithic standing stones, Iron-Age hill forts and medieval churches. He explained this by pointing out that many sites were re-used, so many monuments or buildings would have been built above, say, a long-disappeared Neolithic settlement. Archaeological evidence has shown this is often the case: for example, early Christian churches were often sited over the foundations of pagan temples. However, this can't be verified in every single case.

What about the contention that Watkins' chosen ley lines may ignore sites of similar significance or age that sit just outside a straight line? This too can be countered with the understanding that ancient communities didn't have access to accurate surveying tools, so their straight lines were likely to waver.

An argument in favour of ley lines' existence is that they bear comparisons with similar pilgrim routes discovered abroad. The ancient lines of Nazca and Sajama (pages 227–33) in South America, for example, suggest the desire to link notable locations with straight ritual paths came naturally to pre-modern cultures. Some fringe ideas have arisen to explain the ley lines. In 1961, in his booklet *Skyways and Landmarks*, former RAF pilot Tony Wedd claimed they were laid out by prehistoric people to guide visiting extraterrestrials.

The British author and esotericist John Michell's 1969 book *The View Over Atlantis* helped to reinvigorate interest in ley lines. Michell claimed that the lines followed the path of Earth's energies, with 'telluric [terrestrial] lines of force that ran invisibly across countries, their routes marked above ground by megaliths and tumuli [burial mounds]'. He produced evidence of what he believed was a ley line of extraordinary length running 640 km (400 miles) from St Michael's Mount in Cornwall, south-west England, to Lowestoft on the east coast, via numerous sites associated with the Archangel Michael. However, on close inspection, this path did not prove exactly straight and the sheer number of churches named after St Michael made such a line easy to draw.

A thorough inventory of perceived ley lines was undertaken by Paul Devereux, the British author and Earth mysteries researcher, on becoming editor of the journal *The Ley Hunter* in 1976. He gathered details of all published and unpublished lines shared by readers, weeded out weaker submissions, and published a definitive list of 41 'admissable' ley lines in *The Ley Hunter's Companion* in 1979. Some of these routes genuinely seemed to involve the deliberate positioning of sites in lines rather than accidental alignments.

One of the most convincing of these ley lines involved three Bronze-Age stone spires outside Boroughbridge in North Yorkshire: at around 6 m (20 ft) tall, the 'Devil's Arrows' are some of the tallest such stones in Britain. They were raised between 1800 and 1200BCE in a row 170 m (560 ft) long. Extending this line in both directions passes the remains of Cana Henge and Hutton Moor Henge in one direction and, in the other, henges at Nunwick and

Thornborough. These henges (ring-shaped earthen enclosures) all date from the later Neolithic period (*c.*3000–2500BCE).

Archaeologists and historians were not convinced by this list. Indeed, statistical data has been used to show that alignments between ancient and modern sites were coincidental and that almost any common subject, from post offices to telephone boxes, could be shown to lie on direct paths. In 2010, Matt Parker, from the School of Mathematical Sciences at Queen Mary University of London, produced a map locating branches of the department store Woolworths and showed how easy it was to produce straight lines and equilateral triangles between them.

Standing stone on a ley line, New Radnor, Wales.

## A NEW VIEW OF THE ANCIENT LANDSCAPE

In response to doubts, Devereux published a revised list of ley lines in 1994, but by this point interest had waned. Instead, from the 1980s, a new term was being used to describe concentrations of Neolithic (4000–2500BCE) and Early Bronze Age (2500–1500BCE) ceremonial monuments, the 'ritual landscape'. These arrangements involved congregations of sites surrounding a major feature, such as a 'long barrow' or burial mound. Many of these sites were connected by earthworks such as ditches and causeways.

Cursuses are Neolithic banks and ditches in parallel that can stretch for over 1.5 km (1 mile). They are hard to spot from the ground as they become eroded, but from the air more than 50 have been discovered. The Dorset Cursus in south-west England is about 10 km (6 miles) in length; it forms a wide, curving path that connects two long barrows. It has been suggested that the cursus may have been used for ceremonial processions. Another cursus links burial sites near Stonehenge; it forms a long, straight route and passes other ancient monuments. They are not ley lines, but genuine ancient pathways joining sites of major importance to the Neolithic people who shaped them. It seems that some prehistoric sites were deliberately located within sight or walking distance, with an ordained path between them. While these pathways are not straight or imbued with mystical energy, they are just as fascinating as any engineered ley line.

'New-Age' theories of cosmic energies and ancient paths serving as UFO landing strips were far from Alfred Watkins' original concept. His simple idea that England's ancient sites might be connected with straight trading or ceremonial routes has been embellished with mystic beliefs and pseudoscience. His straight lines have also been superseded by the discovery of cursuses and sprawling ritual landscapes. True or not, fascination with ley lines is destined to last: *The Old Straight Track* and *The Ley Hunter's Manual* are still in print a century after their publication.

A road route between many of the Herefordshire sites that Alfred Watkins sought to link includes Blackwardine, where a commemorative stone has been placed to mark where Watkins came up with his ley line concept, and Woolhope, where he first shared his ideas. The route is circular, rather than straight, but is fittingly named Watkins Way. While Watkins may not have been able to convince archaeologists that his ley lines were key to understanding the English landscape, he did at least succeed in sparking many people's interest in the mysteries of the earth, and in exploring the countless ancient landmarks of the countryside he loved.

# INDEX

# PICTURE CREDITS

**Alamy:** 28, 80, 130, 162, 185, 203, 250

**Getty Images:** 115, 151, 155, 237

**Science Photo Library:** 16

**Shutterstock:** 39, 42, 47, 50, 59, 67, 72, 74, 84, 90, 97, 100, 106, 110, 113, 119, 137, 142, 144, 171, 179, 190, 199, 212, 219, 228, 242

**Wikimedia Commons:** 34